GOATMAN: FLESH OR FOLKLORE?

J. Nathan Couch

Copyright © 2014 J. Nathan Couch
All rights reserved. No part of this publication may be reproduced or transmitted in any form or by any means, electrical or mechanical, including photocopy, recording, or any information storage or retrieval system, without the permission of the author.
Library of Congress Control Number: 2014912547
CreateSpace Independent Publishing Platform
North Charleston, South Carolina
ISBN-10: 1500144533
ISBN-13: 978-1500144531
Printed in the United States by CreateSpace

Published by J. Nathan Couch
West Bend, Wisconsin
E-mail: wcwiparanormalproject@yahoo.com
Website: www.jnathancouch.com

Front Cover painted by Amber Michelle Russell
Exterior and Logo Design by Charlie Hintz of Mental Shed Studios

DEDICATION

This book is dedicated to Eugene Wendleborn, and Jim Borusky, two great men who've embarked on the ultimate adventure. This world is a lesser place without them.

TABLE OF CONTENTS

Acknowledgements · vii
Introduction · ix
Chapter 1   A Satyr in Southeastern Wisconsin · · · · · · · · · · · · · 1
Chapter 2   The Rise and Demise of Satyrs · · · · · · · · · · · · · · · ·18
Chapter 3   Goatman's Grave · 30
Chapter 4   Maryland's Ax-Weilding Genetic Freak · · · · · · · · · · 33
Chapter 5   Fishy Man-Goat of Lake Worth · · · · · · · · · · · · · · · 47
Chapter 6   Texas's Hooved Hoard · 54
Chapter 7   The Ghost at Goatman's Bridge · · · · · · · · · · · · · · · 60
Chapter 8   Little Darling · 69
Chapter 9   California's Beast of Billiwhack · · · · · · · · · · · · · · · · 72
Chapter 10 Keep Off Louisville's Trestle of Death · · · · · · · · · · · 79
Chapter 11 Pennsylvania's Sheepman Runs Amok · · · · · · · · · · · 89
Chapter 12 Sheepsquatch · 94
Chapter 13 A Death in Indiana · 99
Chapter 14 The Shawnee Goat and Other Hoaxes · · · · · · · · · · ·103
Chapter 15 Purgatory, Michigan ·110
Chapter 16 The Mystery Solved? ·113
Chapter 17 But the Monsters Remain ·120

J. Nathan Couch

Timeline of Reported Creature Sightings in the
United States Organized by State ·127
Media Guide ·139
Selected Bibliography ·143
About the Author ·149
Ordering and Contact Information ·151

ACKNOWLEDGEMENTS

A lot of people and organizations around the country made this book possible. Without their kind assistance, this book would have ended up as a pamphlet instead.

From the Fortean community, I owe a great debt to Linda S. Godfrey, Mark Opsasnick, Ken Gerhard, Nick Redfern, Kurt McCoy, Sean Whitley, Dr. Karl P. N. Shuker, Johnathan Moore, Heidi Kirclich LaDow, and Loren Coleman for allowing me to paraphrase from their work, utilize their knowledge, and for putting me into contact with the right people. Much of my original research would have been unachievable without the aid of a lot of extremely helpful people.

From Wisconsin, I'd like to thank Eugene Wendleborn, the West Bend Community Memorial Library, and Heather Pryzbylski and the rest of the Washington County Historical Society staff.

Down in Texas, I'd like to thank Suzanne Fritz at the Fort Worth Central Library, Chuck A. Voellinger at the Denton Public Library, the kind people at the Lake Worth Area Historical Society, and Demented Darling, for all the help in La Porte, Texas.

In other parts of the country, thanks go out to the University of Maryland Folklore Archives, the Indiana State University Folklore Archives, the St. Joseph's County Historical Society (Michigan), and to Dr. Erika Brady at Western Kentucky University.

Thanks to all the Downtown West Bend Ghost Walk patrons whose ticket purchases assisted in financing this project.

Without the exterior design work and website design skills of Charlie Hintz and Mental Shed Studios, this project could not have succeeded.

My infinite gratitude goes out to Eau Claire, WI, artist Amber Michelle Russell. Never has Goatman looked so terrifying *and* utterly charming than on this cover.

Last but not least, I appreciate the critiques of Jessica and Catherine Sawinski, and Sarah Phillips, and the hard work of my editor Katie Harrison. All the red ink was very helpful.

INTRODUCTION

Anyone who authors a book of this nature will invariably be asked one particular question by his or her audience: How did you become interested in such a strange topic? I recall vividly the first time it occurred to me that there might be monsters hiding in the night.

While growing up in the foothills of Georgia's Blue Ridge Mountains, my family lived in a small single-floor home on a curvy, narrow two-lane road. Our "neighborhood" back then consisted of a dozen or so homes separated alternately by tracts of trees and pastures. The only other structures nearby were a small gas station out on the highway, a couple of churches, and an auction house that'd taken over a ramshackle barn across the street from our home. During the time when the story I'm about to tell occurred, my parents had part-time jobs at the auction's snack bar, grilling burgers for rural bargain hunters.

At the time this story takes place, I was roughly six years old. My big sister was nearly twenty, so she was regularly saddled with babysitting. It was a particularly sweltering summer night when I was traumatized. We were too poor to afford air conditioning. Our only salvation from stifling summer nights was box fans, open windows, and screened doors, so sounds from outside entered our home with astounding ease, even over the symphony of noise I usually created as I tried to entertain myself—and to drive Sis batty. Suddenly my obnoxious play was interrupted by piercing shrieks from the woods that abutted our property. I'll never forget the sound. It was like a woman screaming in terror, except not quite human. The noise persisted for what seemed like an eternity, and each scream seemed to get closer. My sister and I were terrified. She telephoned Dad—when she probably should have called the police. He ran home and met us at the front door. Knowing our father knew how to use the small arsenal of hunting rifles locked away in the house, we were instantly reassured. We ventured out onto the lawn with him and listened to the terrible sounds. The screams were now fading away into the darkness.

Dad tried to comfort and assure us that no one was being hurt. He insisted that it was only a panther—pronounced pain'er higher up in the mountains. Little did he know that Sis had recently read to me from a bound edition of *Foxfire*, relating nearly forgotten Appalachian folktales about bloodthirsty panthers creeping through windows on the scent of newly born babies. At the time, these stories hadn't bothered me, since she'd assured me at the outset that panthers had long since vanished from northern Georgia. I don't think I slept a wink that night, and I know I slept with my window closed for a long time indeed, despite the smothering summer nights.

The strange screams would return a year later, this time in the woods on the opposite side of our property. Whatever was making these bloodcurdling sounds seemed to be following the creek that came down from the mountain behind our home. Every dog within five miles bayed and howled as if the devil himself was walking the earth. My visiting aunt joked that it sounded like the wails of a ghost—yet another sleepless night for young me.

Though nearly thirty years have passed since that night, and I now live some eight hundred miles away from where those events took place, I remember them vividly, and I still occasionally wonder, was that just a panther, or something even more sinister?

Long ago my anxiety evolved into unbridled fascination. I've spent a large portion of my life researching—and occasionally investigating—unexplained phenomena of various sorts, but the subject of monsters has remained very dear to me. Needless to say, I was delighted when I first learned of the Goatman—a half-man, half-goat monster that reportedly lives in the hills near my Wisconsin home.

Of course, ever since the advent of electricity, we've all been told—beginning at a very early age—that there are no such things as monsters, that there's nothing out there in the darkness other than the creatures we invent with our own imaginations. Yet, there are encounters out there that suggest otherwise. Hundreds, if not thousands, of people from all around the world, from nearly every religion, ethnicity, and social background, come forward each year claiming they've seen a monster.

These people bravely risk being ostracized to tell the world they've seen Bigfoot walking through their backyard, or an enormous serpent writhing in the lake down the street from their office. These are encounters that can cause even the most open-minded person to raise an eyebrow and wonder about their validity, but encounters such as these seem pedestrian when compared to encountering a half man, half goat. Even in the realm of monster hunting, this book's monster of choice is considered exceedingly strange and extracts outright contempt from certain individuals in the world of unexplained mysteries.

Goatman is considered by many to be such an impossible creature that even entertaining such a notion is a disservice to slightly more probable, but equally implausible monsters, such as the aforementioned lake serpents or Bigfoot.

But despite being an impossibility, Goatman and creatures similar to it have been seen numerous times over the decades, and these sightings should not be ignored. Of course, just because people claim to see Goatman doesn't mean it should be accepted as reality either.

Goatman's biggest problem is that the creature always has an origin myth attached to him that reeks of stale movie theater popcorn, and the moldering pulp of cheesy comic books. In other words, it couldn't be anything more than fantasy. But beneath it all, could there really be a goat-man out there, lurking in the night? I suppose you could say this book is my attempt to illuminate that night—to shine a metaphorical flashlight on all the bunk in the hopes of uncovering a small grain of truth. This book is meant to answer a question only a few have ever asked out loud—is the Goatman flesh, or folklore?

Before you proceed, there is a little you should know regarding how I've chosen to spell this monster's name. Whenever the capitalized "Goatman" appears, it is referring specifically to a version of the creature that's proper name is Goatman, the most famous example being Maryland's Goatman. I use the capitalized spelling in this introduction because I'm referencing the titular creature.

The generic term for goatlike creatures that aren't known properly as Goatman is "goat-man" or "goat-men."

At one point in the book, when discussing a historical figure nicknamed "Goat Man," I retained this particular spelling out of historic significance.

Lastly, some goat-men discussed go by multiple names. For instance, a Louisville, Kentucky, monster is known as "the Pope Lick Monster," "Sheepman," and "Goatman." In instances like this, I've attempted to use the most popular regional name for the sake of clarity. In this instance the Louisville creature is referred to mainly as the Pope Lick Monster.

CHAPTER 1
A SATYR IN SOUTHEASTERN WISCONSIN

It's said all across the United States that a monster lurks in the darkness. But unlike the fearsome beasts of long ago, it doesn't prowl near a secluded crossroads, nor does it lurk in the vast wilderness that once shrouded much of America's landscape. This monster lurks on the boundaries of suburban America. It lives under our bridges, along our highways, in our parks, and in abandoned buildings mere miles from our schools—from our homes. Huge, malodorous, and homicidal, it has many regional monikers, but most people refer to the creature by a singularly powerful, straightforward name—Goatman.

I first learned of Goatman shortly after moving to West Bend, Wisconsin, in 2007. One night in October, I attended a Washington County Historical Society Halloween event called "Ghosts of Washington County." That night the bill included a presentation by a group of paranormal investigators, a costume contest, a play based on the writings of Edgar Allan Poe, and for the grand finish, ghost stories. As the evening drew to a close, local storytellers took turns spinning the sorts of yarns you'd expect to hear in any community—poltergeists at the local university, and a smattering of haunted farmhouses. But the last story of the night was about something entirely unique. The storyteller described a half man, half goat. In her own words, it was a mythological satyr. Now they had my attention! It isn't often someone claims that a creature from Greek mythology resides in present-day Wisconsin—or anywhere else for that matter.

What follows is my retelling of the legend as I remember it from that night. According to the story, Washington County's monster-in-residence was first encountered in the early 1870s by two newlyweds who dared to navigate treacherous Hogsback Road at night. Hogsback Road is located near the tiny unincorporated community of Hubertus, roughly fifteen miles to the south of West Bend. The road is built along a narrow, winding glacial esker formed at the end of the last ice age. The road is a gauntlet of sharp curves and steep hills that snake high above the fields and forests below. Even today the road is hazardous to fatigued or careless motorists.

Despite the risks, the couple drove on in their wagon heedless of the perils that lay ahead, keen to reach their new home. Ultimately, one of their wheels splintered, leaving them stranded in the wilderness. Upon inspection, the husband realized the break was beyond his ability to mend, and professed he'd walk back to town and return with help. His wife was scared—not only to be left alone and vulnerable in such an isolated locale, but for her husband's safety. Bears, wolves, and cougars still prowled southeastern Wisconsin in those days. Her husband, however, wasn't afraid. He assured her that he'd learned more than enough survival skills during service in the Civil War, and that he'd return safely.

Time passed. Night trudged onward. She began to fear the worst. Eventually, she heard movement outside in the dark. It sounded as if a person was approaching. As she neared the canopy of the wagon to greet her lover, she stopped and stood deathly still. She began to hear strange sounds like she'd never heard before. First, heavy snuffling, like a large animal that detected an unfamiliar scent, and then, a coarse bleating like some terrible goat. She cautiously peeked outside, and a terrible form stood in the moonlight. It was a creature covered in coarse red hair standing on two legs like a man, but with the horned head and long muzzle of a goat. She screamed and shrank to the back of the wagon. The animal bleated again, and then there was silence. Time passed. Eventually, through sheer exhaustion, fitful sleep overcame the woman.

The sun was freshly risen when she woke. Galvanized by daylight, she ran outside for any sign of her husband. On the ground, she found large, cloven-hoofed tracks that turned from the wagon and disappeared into the tree line. Bolstered by daylight, she followed. There, at the edge of the forest, the ground around a large oak tree was drenched in blood. She looked up to find the mutilated remains of the man she'd just married dangling from a gnarled limb.

That night the monster learned stranded travelers make for easy prey. Nowadays, the Goatman—who can move so quickly he can scarcely be seen—runs in front of oncoming cars, forcing motorists to veer off the road. If the plunge to the countryside below doesn't kill them, the Goatman will. The cars are always found empty, their passengers dragged away by the monster, never to be found.

The story was blood-spattered, scary, and—as far as I was concerned—perfect. While the Goatman sounded more like an urban legend than an actual paranormal manifestation, something about it appealed to me in a way few other stories ever had. After the program concluded, I knew had to go out in search of the Goatman. The streetlights of West Bend soon faded behind me. I spent nearly an hour driving down lonely back roads looking for the lair of this murderous animal, but I was so unfamiliar with the area, I never even found the correct road, much less Goatman. Though my initial expedition ended in utter failure, the night had been magnificent fun.

As months passed and my number of trips to Hogsback Road began to pile up, my interest began to transcend mere legend tripping, and grow nearly into an obsession. I wanted to know everything I could about the Goatman, including the thing's role within my new community. I soon learned that if you sit around a bonfire in Washington County long enough, you'll hear the legend of the Goatman. While the creature is blamed for causing car accidents so it can steal the bodies of its unfortunate victims, teens and adults alike routinely cruise the countryside in search of the beast.

The Goatman's origin tale may seem familiar to you even if you'd never even heard of the monster until now. Legends such as the Goatman's are often considered "Lovers' Lane legends" by folklorists due to the numerous elements they share with more well-known legends, such as the "Dead Boyfriend." The Dead Boyfriend legend always involves a young couple in seclusion. Their vehicle either runs out of gas and they begin making out to pass the time, or they've gone to a lonely location with the sole intent of being intimate. Some circumstance—usually an odd noise outside—convinces the boy to investigate. After the boy fails to return, the girl sees a shadowy stranger moving in the darkness and locks herself inside. Eventually she hears a dripping noise on the roof of the car. Too terrified to leave the vehicle, the girl waits for daylight. When daylight returns, she goes outside to look for her lover, only to find he's been hanged by his neck above the car, the roof covered in his blood. One version of the Goatman legend archived at Wisconsinosity.com and written by two high school students from the town of Slinger uses this same ending verbatim.

A similar story is the equally well-known Hook Man legend, which itself is believed to have spawned the Dead Boyfriend tale. The story usually begins when a parked teenage couple's make-out session is interrupted by an urgent news flash over the radio. The newscaster warns that a crazed killer has escaped from a local insane asylum. His most distinguishing feature is having a hook in place of his missing hand. The girl immediately becomes frightened and demands to go home. Her boyfriend protests, until they hear a noise outside and he concedes. When they arrive at the girl's home, they discover a huge hook dangling from the passenger side door. Alternate versions of this legend end with the boyfriend being murdered and hanged above the car, an obvious amalgamation with the Dead Boyfriend legend.

Interestingly enough, I spoke with a Hartford, Wisconsin, man who recalls a murderous "Hook Man" who was once said to live on Hogsback Road in an old dilapidated house with a tin roof. Hook Man would use his hook to cut the throats of any teens he caught making out nearby, providing a direct link—or at least a clear correlation—between Goatman and other Lovers' Lane legends. One or two individuals who grew up in the area have even said Goatman was supposed to have lived in the house, rather than the Hook Man.

The Goatman legend does seem to deserve its Lovers' Lane classification. Numerous longtime residents of Washington County recall a time when Hogsback Road was a favored location for optimistic boys to bring their sweethearts for a few minutes of privacy. The Goatman has two other haunts in the county as well: the Jackson Marsh in Jackson, and South Mill Road in Kewaskum—more popularly known as Goatman's Road—both of which were at one point in time also known as secluded teenage make-out locations. Many in the community I interviewed believe that the Goatman was concocted by parents to keep their daughters closer to home—somewhere they'd be obliged to preserve their modesty for as long as possible.

If the legend was in fact created by parents as some peculiar, passive-aggressive form of birth control, it didn't seem to work. Often the only thing more alluring to teenagers than sex is danger, especially the sort of fantastic danger offered by such a far-fetched entity as the Goatman. Going out in search of the creature to impress one's girlfriend became a regular pastime for local boys, and if the creature failed to appear, well, you may as well allow nature to take its course.

Pranks and vandalism involving the Goatman became common. Numerous forty- and fifty-somethings from around Washington

County recall a massive, gnarled old oak tree on Hogsback Road that they referred to as "the hanging tree." This tree, according to legend, was supposed to be the tree where the Goatman stowed his original victim that dark, terrible night. I spoke with several West Bend men who recall leading female classmates on late-night walks to the tree in the 1970s, while an accomplice lay in wait nearby to deliver a fright. One group actually hanged a dummy by a noose to scare several classmates. One Hartford woman informed me that effigy hangings at the tree became a Halloween tradition. Others recalled how the tree became covered in crudely spray-painted pentagrams by the 1980s, implying the Goatman may have taken on satanic connotations in some circles. The poor old oak was eventually cut down because of all of the negative attention it attracted. The Goatman claimed another victim.

While all evidence seems to suggest the Goatman legend originated as a means to deter pubescent experimentation, the notion just didn't work for me—at least not concerning the present-day version of the legend. The Goatman's first victims weren't teenage lovers, but a young married couple. They committed no sin—at least none stated in the story. Their one mistake was traveling a perilous road after dark and being unprepared for a breakdown. The Goatman doesn't even specifically target couples—at least not on Hogsback. He preys on unsuspecting travelers. The Goatman doesn't seem to be a cautionary tale about sex so much as it's about hot-rodding. More than one person who grew up in the area in the 1970s recalls that the largest hill on Hogsback was the scene of many accidents. If you drive down the hill with enough speed, your car can actually leave the ground momentarily. It wasn't uncommon for drivers to build up too much momentum and rocket over the edge of the road. Many people have told me the landscape down below was once littered with the ruins of cars from the fifties and sixties, though if the vehicles are still there, the forest has concealed them. Perhaps as society's attitude about sexuality changed in the United States during the sexual revolution of the 1960s, so did the function of the Goatman? It certainly seems the legend's focus has shifted from chastity belts to safety belts.

There does seem to be a small movement within Washington County to reign in the blood and horror associated with the area's most dreaded monstrosity. On November 11, 2006, the *West Bend Daily News* ran an article entitled "Goatman Goes Environmentalist." The article states that Silverbrook Elementary School teacher Rich Koenings had been telling the Goatman legend at the school's educational camp for what at that time had amounted to twenty-six years. According to Koenings, the legend had changed from terrifying to comforting, at least at YMCA Camp Matawa. The kid-friendly Matawa version claims the Goatman is a human hermit who lives in the Kettle Moraine Forest. This Goatman was said to be a friendly guardian of the forest—motivations a bit truer to the mythological satyr's function as a nature spirit—but he detests litterbugs. Supposedly, if the Goatman finds out someone has been littering, he'll make his presence known by ringing the dinner bell to signal he's looking for the culprit. The article doesn't specify what punishment the Goatman would hand out to these thoughtless children, though the incorporation of ringing a dinner bell seems to imply unspoken insinuations of some Hansel and Gretel–style cannibalism, though perhaps I'm just warped from watching too many George Romero films.

The original version is far less charming. The version the Matawa campers tell each other around the camp's fire goes as follows: Before the camp was built, the land belonged to a lonely old goat farmer. Sometime around the Great Depression of the 1930s, disease wiped out his entire heard. To prevent the spread of sickness to his neighbors' livestock, he dug a huge pit and built a bonfire. With each corpse he threw into the fire, his frustration and anger built. He tossed the final goat into the flames with such rage that he fell into the pit and was burned alive. Now his angry ghost haunts the camp, occasionally taking out his frustrations on unwitting campers—heartwarming, huh?

Of course, all of my speculation about the advent of the legend has assumed that it doesn't have a basis in a real-life encounter. Hogsback Road has been around a very long time, appearing on plat maps around the time the Goatman allegedly made its first kill. The story could actually have originated because of an accident or murder that occurred long ago, very close to the Goatman's legendary genesis in the 1870s. It's certainly in the realm of possibility. Also, perhaps someone was killed by an ordinary animal and it was either misidentified, or over a hundred years of reciting, became mutated into a bogeyman story. Then, of course, there is a chance the Goatman was actually born out of an actual unexplainable encounter like those that occurred in Washington County and surrounding areas in the mid-2000s.

On November 6, 2006, Washington County made national news when Milwaukee TV stations WTMJ and WISN reported that Bigfoot had been sighted near Holy Hill in Hubertus—a location roughly three miles from Hogsback Road and right in the heart of Goatman territory. Bigfoot is the name of perhaps the most well-known "monster" in North America. Sightings of this enormous, manlike ape became worldwide news after frequent sightings in the American Pacific Northwest during the late 1950s and throughout the 1960s. While Bigfoot aficionados use the term specifically to reference sightings of anomalous, hairy bipeds in California, Oregon, Washington State, and the western provinces of Canada, pop culture uses it to describe almost any large mystery ape. It should also be noted that these strange animals have been reported in all forty-eight continental states, Alaska, and every province of Canada. The Holy Hill story quickly went national and became a minor media circus, even being mentioned briefly on CNN. The incident was researched thoroughly by Wisconsin author Linda S. Godfrey, who is an expert on strange creature sightings throughout the American Midwest.

Linda writes about the incident extensively in her book, *Strange Wisconsin*, as well as in the sightings log of her website,

BeastOfBrayRoad.com. The gentleman who had the experience was a Menasha man named Steven Krueger, a contractor who collected roadkill for the Department of Natural Resources. Godfrey interviewed Krueger and learned that Bigfoot may not have been a Bigfoot at all. Krueger was making his appointed rounds early in the morning of November 6, when he noticed a dead deer on the shoulder of State Highway 167 at approximately one thirty in the morning, just east of Holy Hill Basilica, a famous Catholic shrine located atop the highest hill in the county. The deer wasn't marked for pickup, but he stopped anyway, tossing the freshly dead animal in the back of his work truck.

As he filled out paperwork, Krueger noticed his vehicle begin to shake. When he looked in his rearview mirror, he noticed a large, black-furred animal reaching into the back of the truck, grabbing at the deer with his paw. The creature resembled a bear, except it was much too large—six or seven feet tall—and had a doglike head with a long muzzle and pointed, triangular ears. Krueger only saw the animal for approximately five seconds before speeding away, though not before the animal pulled the dead deer and an aluminum ATV ramp from the truck. Krueger returned roughly twenty minutes later to retrieve the ramp, only to discover the deer, the creature, and the ramp were nowhere in sight. In order to avoid ridicule, Krueger didn't plan to report the incident but, by the end of his shift, decided the large animal could be dangerous. Krueger states that he took great care not to say the word "Bigfoot" while reporting the incident to the Washington County Sheriff's Department, but a baffled and/or amused deputy recorded it as a "yeti sighting" nonetheless. Krueger emphatically stated to Godfrey, "It wasn't a 'Bigfoot.'" Godfrey believes this animal to be a "bearwolf"—a bizarre hybrid animal that has allegedly been spotted on occasion in the Wausau area of north-central Wisconsin.

After the initial sighting, many individuals came forward with new or previously unreported sightings. Painting contractor Rick Selcherk told WISN about a November 2004 sighting in which a strange animal crossed the road in front of him on Highway 60 between Slinger and Mayfield. Strange Wisconsin records numerous other sightings. In 1996, two six to seven-foot-tall bipedal, furry creatures with slanted eyes were seen crossing Scenic Road from a cemetery, a mere quarter of a mile from Holy Hill. The witness, identified only as RAS, stated the animals moved very quickly. Others also came forward with sightings from as far away as Merton in Waukesha County, Watertown in Dodge County, and Portage in Columbia County.

Several researchers conducted investigations of the Holy Hill area. A local researcher named Mike Lane investigated the site the day the story broke and found large, bipedal, undefined footprints, but they were too shallow to cast or describe. Lane did find evidence that something large had been sleeping in a nearby barn in a hay pile. Godfrey accompanied Lane on a second uneventful excursion. Despite Godfrey's bruin/canine theory, the shadow of Bigfoot still loomed dark and heavy. Controversial West Coast Bigfoot hunter and Las Vegas promoter Tom Biscardi conducted several hunts right after the initial sighting. It should be noted that Biscardi's legitimacy has been called into question by those in the cryptozoological field on more than one occasion. For those unfamiliar, cryptozoology is the study of unknown species of animals. Biscardi was involved in several high-profile Bigfoot hoaxes in 2005 and 2008, both involving the supposed unveiling of a Bigfoot or its corpse, though he claims that he himself was hoaxed on both occasions.

An article titled "Creature's Identity Questioned" appeared in the November 23, 2006, *Hartford Times Press* and featured opinions from both Godfrey and Biscardi. Biscardi found no evidence that could be analyzed, but did find a "tree twist," something that he identified as a Bigfoot territorial marking. Biscardi theorized the creature had likely left the area, as it had reportedly been shocked by an electric fence in the Waukesha County sighting. Biscardi stated that these animals move very quickly, and that they are often only seen via peripheral vision, like in an encounter he'd recently had in Paris, Texas. This characteristic did remind me of the alleged uncanny speed of the Goatman.

In Godfrey's book *Hunting the American Werewolf*, she points out that oftentimes these strange, unidentified canine creatures are seen near areas sacred to Native Americans, implying a potential supernatural connection. Holy Hill was once a spiritual center for the native Potawatomi people long before Europeans and Catholicism arrived. That's why I believe the most interesting sighting recorded in *Strange Wisconsin* occurred on November 12, 2006, outside of West Bend, near Farmington, just a day after the Krueger sighting made the news. Two men were driving north down Shalom Drive at approximately eight thirty at night when a large, muscular, furry quadruped shambled across the road in front of them. It had a huge round head, pointed ears, no tail, and was the size of a deer. Shalom Drive is located less than three miles from Lizard Mound County Park. Lizard Mound contains dozens of puzzling Native American effigy mounds. The location is said to be haunted, but most unique of all, local tradition says that on supernaturally significant nights such as Halloween, or during full moons, the spirits of the Mound Builders are supposed to be active, often accompanied by a fearsome beast. There was a full moon on November 12, 2006. While it certainly isn't proof that this was a paranormal event, it is an intriguing coincidence.

I'm certain by now some of you have decided that rather than a Bigfoot or a bearwolf, the strange animal being seen is likely just a misidentified bear. While there are no longer any species of bears in southeastern Wisconsin, black bear populations are booming in northern Wisconsin, and these large predators are gradually moving south. In 2010, a black bear made its way through Washington County but was eventually captured and relocated a few days later, when it showed up uninvited in Ozaukee County at Port Washington's annual street festival Pirate Fest. A black bear could explain sightings of unusual quadrupeds but not the two-legged variety. Bears rarely walk on two feet. Even when the strange creature was only seen on all fours, witnesses claimed familiarity with bears and were adamant that what they had seen was not a known type of bruin.

Reports of the creature(s) are still trickling in. As I researched my previous book, *Washington County Paranormal: A Wisconsin Legend Trip*, a woman named AJ contacted me about a possible bearwolf sighting that occurred in June, 2006—a full five months before the Krueger sighting. Her story appeared in that book and is summarized here. Her two young sons and a friend were playing in the Silver Creek area near Washington Avenue in West Bend, when they chased a fox or cat into a swampy, wooded area. When they finally found the animal, it was being eaten by a large, tailless, canine creature with red eyes. The red-eyed creature was crouched over the dead animal on two legs. The kids weren't scared of it despite the fact that it looked them in the eyes—normally an indication of aggression. AJ's kids said the animal was "a lot bigger than Grandpa," a man who stood six feet four. AJ didn't believe the kids and incredulously dismissed it as a carnie from a nearby church festival wearing a fur coat—a farfetched explanation to say the least. Once the Krueger sighting broke, she believed the children weren't mistaken. I also heard from secondhand reports that a large black quadruped was seen eating a dead turkey outside the Washington County city of Kewaskum in February, 2012. When alarmed motorists slammed on the breaks to avoid hitting the creature, the animal allegedly ran away into the woods on two legs.

After *Washington County Paranormal* was published, other people have come forward with sightings. Once while dining in Downtown West Bend, a member of the restaurant staff told me of an encounter he had with Bigfoot during the 2006 Holy Hill furor—a sort of welcome dinner interruption I've become accustomed to. He couldn't remember the date, but it wasn't long after the November 2006 sightings. He was at a friend's home along a wooded area near Holy Hill when something slammed against the side of the house with such a tremendous force that it knocked all the pictures off the wall. When his friend opened the door to sick his dogs on whomever or whatever was outside, the dogs cowered in the corner and refused to go outside.

On May 3, 2012, I was contacted via Facebook by a man who excitedly claimed his girlfriend had sighted Bigfoot near the Horicon Marsh in neighboring Dodge County at approximately ten forty that night. The gentleman had promised to contact me with details after he left work, but despite my numerous attempts to contact him, he never replied. My assumption is his girlfriend muzzled him regarding the incident.

In October, 2013, during a paranormal history tour I was guiding in Downtown West Bend, a family told me about an unusual set of footprints they'd discovered in their front yard near the Pike Lake area, in Hartford, Wisconsin. Pike Lake is located about ten miles southeast of Holy Hill. On Christmas morning in 2009, the woman's husband discovered a set of humanlike footprints in the snow, but they were much too large to belong to a person. The prints measured some fifteen inches from heel to toe, but what was even more puzzling was that the prints appeared to have six toes. The family photographed the prints, which were covered by a fresh snowfall within ten minutes of discovery. Alarmed, the family called the Department of Natural Resources. When an officer looked at the photographs, he said similar tracks had been spotted around Pike Lake. The officer theorized they were made by "faulty snowshoes." The family didn't agree. The home is located about a quarter of a mile into the woods, and they've never known of anyone venturing so deep into the woods on snowshoes. The matriarch of the family admits that perhaps the tracks were some strange fluke, considering their dogs had been playing in the yard prior to the discovery of the tracks, but she'll never believe they were made by snowshoes.

While Godfrey's research pointed toward a more canine-like creature as the culprit of the 2006 monster flap, her 2011 book, *Monsters of Wisconsin,* contains an incident that describes an undeniably Bigfoot-like creature near Holy Hill. A gentleman named Ross Tamms related an incident to Godfrey via e-mail that occurred in the scenic area near Holy Hill in the late 1980s. Tamms and his girlfriend had decided to take a drive one sunny afternoon. As the two passed a rural farmhouse, they noticed a huge reddish-brown-haired animal kneeling, holding a small dead dog. They slowed down and were able to take in more detail. The huge thing had thick fur, broad shoulders, a short, almost nonexistent neck, and a black face similar to a great ape's. Tamms noted the animal had a peculiar, humanlike quality and it seemed to be sad, perhaps over the dog's death. The odor of the animal reached the car as they were driving away—the scent was so strong that the two became nauseated. Despite his girlfriend's wishes to turn around for a second look, Tamm decided the creature should be left to do whatever it was trying to do. This encounter is especially intriguing, as it took place in broad daylight.

The witnesses who have come forward since 2006 create a timeline of more than thirty years in which hairy, bipedal creatures have been seen roaming around the Washington County area. One wonders how many other sightings were never reported. It would be reasonable to assume the Goatman legend sprang from long-ago sightings of these strange animals were it not for one problem—the existence of these furry culprits has yet to be proven.

Interestingly enough, hardly any of the articles about the Bigfoot/bearwolf clamor mentioned the Goatman. I have discovered this is a common occurrence in the realm of the unexplained. The very idea of a goat-man roaming the American Midwest is so absurd that not even die-hard supporters of controversial creatures like Bigfoot will champion the possibility that one could exist. Forteans—those who study unexplained phenomena—usually banish the Goatman to the realm of folklore, which is perhaps where it rightfully belongs. None of the strange creature sightings in Washington County remotely match the description of the Goatman of legend. I, myself, had decided that the legend was only legend, until I interviewed someone who had actually encountered the monster. From there on out my entire perspective changed.

The sighting occurred in Kewaskum in the woods around Goatman's Road. The narrow dirt road is actually called South Mill Road, which dead-ends in the middle of the Milwaukee River Flood Plain Forest not far from the ruins of an old farmhouse in which the Goatman once allegedly lived. It should be noted that Goatman's Road has claim to its own variation of the Goatman legend—though the Hogsback-style origin is still better known in Kewaskum. In the Kewaskum variation, the Goatman is an alcoholic who abused both his wife and livestock. One particularly brutal night, he beat his wife to death, then turned his cruelty toward the goats penned out back. One of the animals managed to mortally wound the lout with its horns, and the farmer bled out in the forest. Too terrible to remain dead, he once again stalks the woods as a violent goatlike abomination. I've looked into the legend and discovered that the old house was moved there in the 1960s by the DNR. After the move, they discovered it was impractical to hook the house up to electricity. The house was soon abandoned and left to ruin. However, it appears something strange does lurk in those woods, according to a lifelong Washington County resident named Jason Miller. Here's his terrifying encounter with the Goatman, as published in *Washington County Paranormal*.

In the autumn of 2003, Jason set up his tree stand off South Mill Road in preparation to enjoy some bow hunting. When he returned to hunt a few days later, he discovered it had been taken down and moved about a hundred yards from its original location. There were marks on it that resembled hoofprints.

Thinking it was a combination of another hunter's prank and the marks of some ordinary animal like a deer, Jason put the stand back in the tree. A few weeks later, he again returned. He sat there, hoping to spy a trophy buck. Instead, he saw something entirely unexpected.

The relative quiet of the forest was disturbed by the sounds of something large approaching, something that sounded angry. Looking off into the thick brush, Jason could hardly believe what shambled into the clearing.

"It was the size of a deer, tan and gray in color. It looked like a goat but with a human head and arms. I remember it had a beard that was gray and very long.

"It smelled like rotting flesh and garbage all mixed into one. I remember it was swearing, literally talking under its breath, something about 'trespassers.' What scared me most was the sight of it."

Jason sat in utter shock as he watched the creature, bow at the ready should it notice him in the trees.

Fortunately for Jason, the [Goatman] didn't notice him or was looking for a different "trespasser."

"I didn't waste any time getting out of there. I left as soon as he was out of sight. I kept an arrow nocked 'cause I didn't know what else to do, really. I had heard stories about how violent he can get."

Jason once thought nothing of casually entering those woods, but now?

"I don't like going there anymore...especially not without protection." *Jason's close encounter with the foul-mouthed satyr is likely to remain with him as long as he lives.*

"Eight years later, some of the details are a bit blurry, but I'll never forget what he looked like. I'll never forget."

Just as I thought I was starting to get a firm grasp on the Goatman, along came Jason's story—a wide-awake nightmare. Prior to learning of his experience I had whittled down my self-appointed task to merely explaining the origin of the Goatman legend, and why it exists at all. Once I began to wonder if this creature might actually be real, it seemed the entire scenario changed.

To further complicate my task, it became evident very early into my research that the Goatman was not a creature that belonged solely to Washington County, as I initially assumed. I quickly learned that some Ozaukee residents claimed Goatman lurked in the rural areas around Newburg and in the woods of Saukville's Grady Park. In Fond du Lac County, the beast supposedly lurked around the shores of Auburn Lake. In the Central Wisconsin town of Weyauwega in Waupaca County, the Goatman allegedly made his debut by slaughtering two teens on a "make-out couch" along haunted Marsh Road!

Not only was the Goatman popping up all across Wisconsin, but all across the country. As my research extended beyond Wisconsin, it rapidly became apparent that Washington County's monster was merely one of many hooved horrors dotting American suburbia. It seemed these strange amalgamations from antiquity were everywhere, and I needed to know why.

CHAPTER 2

THE RISE AND DEMISE OF SATYRS

To fully understand Goatman, one needs to understand the mythological beings with which he allegedly has a kinship. More often than not, Goatman is described as a satyr. These days, satyrs are thought of as hairy, humanlike beings with horns and two hooved, goatlike legs, but originally these ancient-Greek nature spirits were depicted in art and story as handsome young men with the long ears and the full, bushy tails of horses. They were most often in the company of the god of wine, Dionysus.

The Roman Empire adopted much of the mythology and deities of Greece, blending it with elements of their own preexisting mythology. Greece's satyrs and Rome's own fauns—similarly bawdy half-man, half-goat nature spirits—would become one and the same in art and literature. It was during this time that the satyr's horselike characteristics became largely forgotten by the general population.

Though sometimes depicted as tricksters with an occasional tendency toward violence, satyrs, whether portrayed as horselike or goatlike, were most often described as drunkards who danced across the landscape lusting after females—both their fellow nature spirits the nymphs as well flesh-and-blood human women.

Another common alias for Goatman is Pan—or his Roman counterpart, Faunus—god of forests, fields, fertility, and music. While Pan is often described as the youngest and most immature of all the Greek gods, he's most likely the oldest. Mythologists and historians know that Pan was worshipped as early as the sixth century BC in Arcadia. Because Pan represents the most simple and primitive needs and desires of humanity, and he's described almost identically as the fauns of Roman myth, he's occasionally been called a satyr in less scholarly literature, despite his status as a god.

Pan is best known for his carnal attraction to the nymphs, especially one named Syrinx. Pan pursued her through the forest, but she turned herself into water reeds to escape his advances. Out of heartbreak—and perhaps a bit of spite—Pan cut down the reeds and made a set of panpipes from which he played a haunting tune.

It should now be easier to understand why Goatman legends in America are often attached to areas where people go to fornicate. Pan, satyrs, and fauns all had reputations for thinking with their, ahem, smaller brain.

While Pan was generally a benevolent god, he—like all ancient Greek gods—had a dark side. Anyone unfortunate enough to disturb his sleep in the wild places of the world would be overcome with a maddening fear. The word panic, if you haven't guessed, is derived from Pan's name.

His ability to induce panic is supposedly what turned the tide in the battle between the gods of Mount Olympus and the Titans, an older race of deities. Pan's earsplitting screams filled the Titans with such a fright that they fled the field of battle.

Considering that Pan was instrumental in the rise to power of the Olympians, it's rather appropriate that his death is also interpreted as their symbolic downfall by certain scholars. Plutarch writes in his *De*

Oraculorum Defectu that as an Egyptian pilot named Thamus was passing by the island of Paxi during the reign of Tiberius, a disembodied voice called to Thamus by name. The strange voice demanded that as he sail past the island of Palodes, he announce Great Pan had died. The pilot did as instructed. Loud cries of anguish erupted from the animals, the plants, and the earth. Numerous writers from the infancy of Christianity view this as the symbolic death of paganism, some even claiming that this event occurred on the same day Christ was nailed to the cross.

Surprisingly enough, though, these ancient ancestors of Goatman have received perhaps more mention in Fortean literature than he has. For those curious, "Fortean" describes anomalous phenomena, and is named after the field's pioneering researcher, Charles H. Fort. Though Goatman is a seemingly American phenomenon, there is insight to be gained from studying satyrs and the remote possibility they once existed.

There are a handful of cryptozoologists and anthropologists who do believe a population of satyrs could have once roamed the Old World, though only a few of them believe they were truly goat-men. The majority of this minority believes that satyrs were either anomalous Neanderthals or a type of protohuman still unknown to science that managed to survive until Hellenistic times.

Dr. Helmut Loofs-Wissowa from the Australian National University's faculty of Asian studies is one such anthropologist. Loofs-Wissowa has an active interest in cryptozoology. He's of the opinion that an intelligent form of primate distinct from all known forms exists in Indochina, and he has been on numerous expeditions in search of these creatures. In a 1994 edition of the scientific journal *Human Evolution*, Loofs-Wissowa referenced the alleged lasciviousness of satyrs as possible evidence that they could have been the last remnant of a Hellenistic Neanderthal population. Loofs-Wissowa points out that most satyrs in classical art are often portrayed as having erect penises even when engaged in nonsexual activities. He theorizes that these upright members could be depictions of a physiological condition called "penis rectus." This condition—which makes the phallus seem erect even when flaccid—is extremely rare in modern humans and has only been recorded in the Bushmen of South Africa. He goes on to reference Paleolithic cave art from Europe that depicts hairy humanoids—possibly Neanderthals—with this provocative affliction. Moving beyond this possible phallic link, he lists the Neanderthal's hairy body, thick neck, large brow, and rounded head as other satyr-like characteristics.

Cryptozoologist Dr. Karl Shuker references Loofs-Wissowa's theory in his book, *The Unexplained*. Shuker points out Loofs-Wissowa's theory fails to explain other satyr physiology such as hooves, tails, or horns found in such art, a fine point indeed.

I personally believe that Loofs-Wissowa's theory isn't all that far-fetched. Remember that the earliest depictions of satyrs were simply wild men with pointed ears and horselike tails. While I won't go so far as to say Neanderthals roamed the woods of ancient Greece, folktales of Neanderthals could easily mutate into tales of fantastic animals over time. After generation upon generation of oral tradition, animal hides worn as loincloths could become horses' tails, which in turn could allow other animallike characteristics such as large ears, and much later, hooves and horns, to enter their descriptions.

On the other hand, cryptozoologist Mark A. Hall believes the mythology of satyrs could have been formed from sightings of an unknown form of ape similar to Asia's Yeti but is descended from the extinct *dryopithecus*. He attributes their goat-man reputation to mistaken perceptions of their extraordinary physical capabilities combined with an unusual form of locomotion.

Hall's theory brought to mind a disquieting encounter tucked away in Ivan T. Sanderson's classic *Abominable Snowmen: Legend Come to Life*, one of the earliest books about Bigfoot-like creatures. While on a 1934 expedition in the Pamir mountain range between the Darvaz Ridge and the western spurs of the Peter the First Mountains in Central Asia in what is now Tajikistan, geologist B. M. Zdorik and his guide had an eerie experience at eight thousand feet in altitude. They reached a level, grassy area where they found evidence of digging, along with drops of blood and a fresh mole skin. Soon they came across a patch of tall wild oats where a creature lay sleeping. It had long, elegant legs with black-soled feet and was covered in a grayish, shaggy fur, similar to a yak's. The creature appeared to be around four feet and ten inches in height and had a smooth back. Unfortunately, the forelimbs and head were obscured by the oats. The relaxed, even heaving of the creature's sides suggested it was sleeping. Zdorik couldn't identify the animal, but he was certain it wasn't any sort of bear. The guide was overtaken by panic, which quickly spread to Zdorik. The two ran as if their lives depended on it, stumbling all the way back down the path. After I learned of the seemingly irrational terror the two men experienced over a sleeping, albeit unfamiliar animal, I couldn't help but be reminded of the myths of Pan, despite the outlandishness of the notion.

The next day the locals learned of the encounter and became alarmed. They used a word to describe the creature that Zdorik apparently couldn't understand, as he said that they started using the word "dev" as a way to make themselves understood. "devs," "daevs," or "divs" are all words used in that part of the world to describe demons or lesser gods. In folklore, Devs are commonly described as having horns and tails, much like European satyrs. The locals described the animals as looking like short, stocky humans that walked upright and were covered in gray fur. They made no mention of horns or tails, and to Zdorik's surprise, made no reference to the supernatural.

That day, Zdorik learned that, though rarely seen, pairs of these creatures lived in the wilds of Sanglakh. In 1933 an adult was supposedly captured while eating grain at a flour mill outside of Tutkaul, Tajikistan. It was chained to the mill for two months, kept alive with meals of raw meat and flour pancakes, until one day the animal broke free and fled back to the wilderness. The locals also stated that no young devs had ever been seen. This point leads one to wonder if the locals were describing a species at the doorsteps of extinction. Perhaps the Dev population had dwindled until there were no longer any viable breeding pairs?

Cryptozoologists in and around the former Soviet Union believe this could have been a specimen of the Russian "Snowman"—also known in China, Mongolia, and surrounding areas as the Alma—a Bigfoot-like creature that continues to be reported in the Pamir region, especially since the word "dev" seems to have only been used for lack of a better term. The fact that the creature's head could not be seen leaves me to wonder if it sported the iconic horns of a satyr. Whatever it was, it remains a frustrating mystery. Whether it was a satyr, a dev, or some other creature entirely, one wonders if Zdorik saw the last specimen of an animal now lost to time.

Beyond this possible satyr sighting, most reports of these creatures come from antiquity. While most of these encounters have been relegated to the realm of myth by nearly everyone except a few branches of modern paganism, a select few examples have earned brief mentions in Fortean literature. What follows is a sampling.

In his *Histories*, Herodotus describes a flayed hide on display in fifth-century-BC Phrygia—now the Turkish city of Dinar—that allegedly had belonged to a satyr named Marsyas, who was killed by the god Apollo after losing a musical contest. According to mythology, Marsyas's blood flowed so heavily that a river was formed. The Marsyas River was a tributary of the Menderes River, which was supposedly formed from the tears of satyrs and nymphs mourning his death. Most—if not all—of this is certainly myth, but the claim that the hide of a satyr acted as a sort of a tourist attraction is a plausible enough claim to make one wonder if at least this portion of the tale is based on some sort of encounter with an extraordinary animal. Of course, we'll never learn if the satyr's skin was authentic, or some ancient hoax.

Plutarch's *Lives* gives the following account of Roman general Lucius Cornelius Sulla's interrogation of a satyr found sleeping in a sacred meadow called Nymphaeum, near Durres in present-day Albania, following the conquest of Athens during the first Mithridatic War.

> *Here, they say, a satyr, such as statuaries and painters represent, was caught asleep, and brought before [Sulla], where he was asked by several interpreters who he was, and, after much trouble, at last uttered nothing intelligible, but a harsh noise, something between the neighing of a horse and crying of a goat. [Sulla], in dismay, and deprecating such an omen, bade it be removed.*

The fifth-century-BC Greek physician Ctesias, in *Indica*, tells of swift-footed satyrs in India that could run on either two or four legs. They were so swift they could only be captured when sickness or old age made it possible. These beings lived in the mountains of a place called Catarcludi, though it should be mentioned that Ctesias also includes anecdotes of an eighteen-foot-tall race of Indians and a species of one-legged men with feet so large, they could lie on their backs and use them as parasols. The latter claim is so far-fetched, I laughed out loud even while researching the most outlandish of Goatman legends.

First-century-AD Roman geographer Pomponius Mela tells of innumerable "goat-pans and satyrs" along the outer coasts of Africa in his *Description of the World*. The land they inhabit is described as a vast, open field, on which there is no trace of civilization, not even a man's footprint, but at night the mountain beyond lights up with their campfires, and their resounding, otherworldly music fills the night. As compelling as this story is, Mela himself writes with a skeptical tone regarding the authenticity of these African goat-men.

Pausanias, a second-century-AD Greek traveler and geographer, had a strong interest in satyrs. After many inquiries he learned this tale, which appears in his *Descriptions of Greece*:

Goatman: Flesh or Folklore?

Euphemus the Carian said that on a voyage to Italy he was driven out of his course by winds and was carried into the outer sea, beyond the course of seamen. He affirmed that there were many uninhabited islands, while in others lived wild men. The sailors did not wish to put in at the latter, because, having put in before, they had some experience of the inhabitants, but on this occasion they had no choice in the matter. The islands were called Satyrides by the sailors, and the inhabitants were red haired, and had upon their flanks tails not much smaller than those of horses. As soon as they caught sight of their visitors, they ran down to the ship without uttering a cry and assaulted the women in the ship. At last the sailors in fear cast a foreign woman on to the island. Her the satyrs outraged not only in the usual way, but also in a most shocking manner.

In other words, they sexually assaulted her. This is certainly a sensational story, and some sensational theories have been offered to explain away a sexual assault by satyrs. In the July-December 1870 edition of *The Month*, Reverend Thomas Meyrick quoted Father Latifeau, who was known for his work regarding Native American customs. In his article, "The Caribees of the Honduras," Latifeau quotes a translation of Pausanias's work that describes the satyrs as having skin of dark red. He theorizes that the sailors had been blown off course as far as the Caribbean, and had encountered native Caribs of the Lesser Antilles Islands, who were known to paint their bodies with red ochre. Of course, one must accept that Euphemus and his fellow Carians accidentally visited the New World 1,300 years before Columbus discovered the Americas, and returned telling tales of satyr rape.

One of Christianity's earliest writers, Saint Jerome, writes of Roman emperor Constantine's trip from Constantinople to the city of Antioch, now the city of Antakya, Turkey, to view the mummified remains of a satyr preserved in salt.

Stanford University's Adrienne Mayor theorizes in her book, *The First Fossil Hunters: Paleontology in Greek and Roman Times*, that this particular satyr could have been a normal human mummy disguised with an elaborate satyr mask like those once used in satyr plays—brief, satirical burlesques—or even a trick of taxidermy.

In the July 23, 2007, *USA Today* article, "Mythical Satyr May Be Preserved in Salt," Mayor points to the then-recent discovery of an ancient Iranian "salt man" in the city of Zanjan as a clue to the origin of the Antioch satyr. Mayor points out that human bodies preserved in salt are peculiar in that the hair of the person usually remains intact, while the skin becomes desiccated. The article shows a photo of the Iranian Salt Man, whose bulging forehead, upturned nose, and strawberry-blond hair and beard are undeniably satyr-like. But much like Marsyas's hide, we'll never know exactly what the strange relic was that caught Constantine's attention.

Early-twentieth-century Scottish psychic, spiritualist, and author Violet Tweedale recounts a particularly intriguing encounter told to her at a party by an alleged eyewitness, the first Lady Henry Grosvenor, born Miss Erskine Wemyss of Wemyss Castle. The following is an excerpt from Tweedale's 1919 book, *Ghosts I Have Seen*.

> *She told us that when a child of seven years old, she had passed through some minutes of such absolute terror that as long as she lived she would never forget the experience. With another child, and a nurse in attendance, she was playing one summer morning out of doors. After a little while the nurse rose from her seat amongst the heather, and wandered away a short distance, out of sight but not out of hearing. A few moments after [that] the two little girls heard some bushes behind them rustling, and a huge creature, half-goat, half-man, emerged and, leisurely crossing the road in front of them, plunged into the woods beyond, and was lost to sight. Both children were thrown into a paroxysm of terror, and screamed loudly. The nurse ran back to them, and when told what was the matter scolded them for their*

foolish fancies. No such animal existed such as they described, an animal much bigger than a goat, that walked upright, and had but two legs, and two hoofs, that was covered with shaggy brown hair from the waist downward, and had the smooth skin of a man from the waist upward! The nurse bade them come home at once, and as they gained the road Miss Wemyss pointed down into the dust. Clearly defined was the track of a two-hoofed creature that had crossed at that spot. The nurse stared for a moment or two, then with one accord they all ran. She never took her charges near that spot again.

Lady Henry said that the memory of that experience was so firmly grafted on her mind that she could always recall with perfect clarity the exact appearance of this appalling creature. In later years, when grown up, she realized from pictures that what she had seen was a faun or satyr. Such pictures or statues always sent a thrill of horror through her. She attributed this apparition to the fact that she and her companion were playing close to the site of a Roman camp, and the road was an old Roman road.

While this story lacks elements of the supernatural beyond a strange creature, another story in *Ghosts I Have Seen* is atypical of the occult writings of the early twentieth century. Nearly all alleged satyr encounters since this time period are of the same sort—exceedingly strange and supernatural. Tweedale writes that a Prince Valori from the continent was alleged to have had a satyr that became attached to him after attending an orgy at a witch's Sabbath in the Vosges Mountains near the German-French boarder. This "familiar" was supposedly with Valori everywhere he went from that moment on, including a party that Tweedale attended. If this satyr ever existed, it was likely some gimmick employed by the aging, unwed continental to marry a wealthy spiritualist heiress, a goal he'd long been attempting to achieve.

An even more eyebrow-raising episode also comes from Scotland, and is chronicled in Robert Ogilvie Crombie's posthumously published book, *The Gentleman and the Faun*. Crombie—also called ROC in New Age circles—regularly visited Edinburgh's Royal Botanical Garden for exercise and meditation, a regiment meant to aid a delicate heart condition. In March, 1966, it was in this garden that ROC claims to have encountered a small faun named Kurmos. ROC first became aware of the three-foot-tall creature as it danced around a tree some twenty yards away. When finished, the peculiar little goat-man sauntered over and sat in front of ROC. When ROC said hello, the little creature jumped with a start, puzzled over how a human could see him. After much conversation, ROC invited the faun to his flat, and a peculiar friendship began.

Eventually, ROC allegedly encountered the god Pan in the same garden while trying to visit Kurmos. ROC described Pan as an enormous faun, taller than himself. After much questioning, ROC admitted a love for Pan and all nature spirits. The story gets stranger and stranger. His next meeting occurred in May of that year on the miniscule island of Iona of the Inner Hebrides. This time Pan appeared to ROC from out of the ground as a faun some twenty-five feet tall. Pan bafflingly identified himself as a servant of the Almighty God. From that point forward, ROC identified himself as a sort of prophet; spreading Pan's message of reconciliation between man and the nature spirits to avoid some terrible ecological calamity.

Outside of alleged experiences like these from spiritualists and occultists at the turn of the last century, encounters with satyrs have been almost nonexistent since antiquity. As Christianity spread throughout Europe, all things pagan were either slowly assimilated into the church or demonized. Satyrs and fauns, much like the gods Pan and Faunus themselves, were lusty and worldly, two characteristics frowned on by the Church. It is no accident that Satan's physical appearance is described as strikingly similar to that of a satyr. If satyrs ever were flesh and blood—which of course remains highly unlikely—I'm certain later sightings would be considered demonic encounters and quickly relegated to the realm of fire and brimstone.

Take for instance this account from Saint Anthony the Great. As Anthony was journeying through the desert to find Saint Paul of Thebes, he claimed to have encountered both a satyr and a centaur in the desert outside of Alexandria, Egypt. Anthony described these creatures as demons. When asked for his identity, the satyr replied, "I am a corpse, one of those whom the heathens call satyrs, and by whom they are snared into idolatry." When the satyr failed to frighten him away, the centaur admitted that the old gods had been overthrown, and the satyr begged for Anthony's blessing. While it's likely this was only propaganda written to win over the last of the pagans, it prophesized the downfall of the mythical satyr almost perfectly.

CHAPTER 3
GOATMAN'S GRAVE

One of the earliest anxieties I can recall from my childhood is the idea that Satan would drag me to hell. This notion was implanted into my impressionable little mind by my devout Baptist grandmother Sybil with the absolute best of intentions. I had done something wrong—what it was, I can't recall, though it likely involved saying a bad word or picking my nose. She told me about another little boy she knew who had once behaved the same as me. When he didn't change his ways, a ring of fire appeared in the floor of his home and the devil rose out of it and spirited him away, never to be seen again.

I'd wager this had a far greater effect on me than she ever knew. It was weeks before I was comfortable being anywhere alone, and even all these years later, when I think of her obviously fictitious cautionary tale, I can vividly picture a horned, diabolical fiend rising from the flames that used to be my childhood bedroom floor, a wicked grin of delight on his tomato-red visage.

But like I said, she meant well.

That exact terrifying scenario has entered my mind many times over during my investigation of the Goatman phenomenon. The Christian church modeled its earliest depictions of the devil's appearance after the satyrs and fauns of paganism, and since the Goatman is often described as one of these nature spirits, the Goatman is—in a roundabout way—a devil. Upon hearing a Goatman story for the first time, far more Americans are likely to picture a demon or the archfiend himself, rather than Pan and his exotic European brethren. With that said, it's no surprise that Goatman legends often cite devil worship as the primary cause of these manifestations.

Old, dilapidated Pine Hill Cemetery in Phelps County, Missouri, is just such an alleged satanic site. Located between the cities of Rolla and St. James, the oldest legible date of death to be found on a Pine Hill tombstone is 1835; however, many of the graves are so old only large rocks mark the locations of their occupants. For years this cemetery has suffered vandalism, littering, and all sorts of indignities because of Missouri's local Goatman legend.

Several graves are covered with large limestone slabs. Folklore says that these plots belong to individuals who were accused of and executed for practicing witchcraft in the late eighteenth and early nineteenth centuries. It's also alleged that satanic rituals continue there to this day. The Internet contains numerous accounts from people who claim to know others who've been chased out of the cemetery by angry occultists. The result of all this supposed devilry is a fearsome, demonic goat-man entity that usually materializes as a pair of fierce, glowing red eyes, leaving enormous cloven hoofprints as it wanders the graveyard by night. This entity enjoys chasing nocturnal trespassers, and occasionally burning holes into their clothing. Because of this alleged entity, Pine Hill is more popularly known within the community as Goatman's Grave.

While I can neither confirm nor deny the existence of malevolent entities or satanic rituals at Pine Hill, the legend of executed witches is easily debunked. The infamous Salem Witch Trials were the last of the officially sanctioned American witch trials, and they ended in 1693. By 1735, witchcraft was no longer punishable by law in Great Britain, and it wasn't until 1844 when the first European-American settler built a home in what is now the city of Rolla. It's extremely unlikely anyone would have been executed for practicing witchcraft in Phelps County, Missouri, not even by vigilantes. Furthermore, those executed for witchcraft were never buried on consecrated ground. To do so would be considered an affront to God.

But it isn't the flimsy framework of the Goatman's Grave legend, nor the hellfire and brimstone manifestations that it alleges that makes the location so interesting. It's the fact that the place is called "Goatman's Grave" and not "Satan's Cemetery," or "The Devil's Boneyard" when the legend is describing, at the very least, what could easily be a foot soldier in Hell's Army. Why the name "Goatman" at all?

I think, perhaps, the simple answer can be found by examining what many blood-and-bone humans do when visiting a location such as Goatman's Grave—drink and fornicate. For lack of a better term—they party. As my little anecdote of boyhood trauma illustrates, the mere idea of the devil is thoroughly frightening. Even if you don't believe in the devil, such an utterly powerful, malign entity is an unsettling idea at the least. It's common knowledge that the goal of the Christian devil is nothing less than the ruination of all that is good, and he often causes it by offering people fleeting, shallow happiness. Such a notion doesn't often inspire promiscuity in a young lad's date, nor does it make anyone particularly thirsty. The name Goatman, on the other hand, is simplistic to the point of absurdity. The devil is a mockery of all that is good, but it seems the Goatman is a mockery of that mockery. The idea of Goatman is too silly to cause serious fright yet familiar enough to offer the illusion of danger—and for a lot of us, danger is fun and sexy. That's a simple answer, though, and those often only apply to simple questions. As I marched forward, I learned that even the most absurd goat-man legend is anything but simple.

CHAPTER 4

MARYLAND'S AX-WEILDING GENETIC FREAK

If the Goatman has a place of birth, it could be Prince George's County, Maryland. In fact, numerous bloggers and wiki editors are certain of it. They state it as fact without so much as offering a reliable source. While such a distinction remains to be proven, Maryland's sinister satyr does have bragging rights. Maryland's beast is without a doubt America's most notorious goat-man. On those occasions when pop-culture has chosen a goat-man as its monster du jour, the story usually takes place in the Free State. Maryland's version has appeared in numerous documentaries, horror films, and comic books. But decades before Maryland's favorite monster was utilized for entertainment, he was a very real terror to the people in and around Bowie, Maryland, a once rural community located in Prince George's County, just outside of sprawling Washington, DC.

The Maryland Goatman's menace reached its pinnacle in the early 1970s. By this point, numerous legends about the creature had proliferated. While some of the legends involve a deranged human hermit, most center on a murderous half-man, half-goat hybrid. The Goatman originally lurked in the woods around Fletchertown Road in Bowie, where it was said he would attack teenage couples or kill pets that wandered into his woods.

The most commonly told origin for Maryland's Goatman involves a US Department of Agriculture (USDA) complex called the Beltsville Agricultural Research Center (BARC). BARC is located about ten miles northeast of Bowie, and is situated on nearly sixty-five hundred acres of land.

According to legend, an unidentified BARC scientist was conducting experiments on goats. The purposes given for these experiments are legion. Some versions of the legend have the doctor searching for eternal youth, while others say he was trying to discover a cure for cancer. One story has him splicing together goat and human DNA seemingly for the hell of it. Regardless of motive, the experiment was botched, resulting in a mockery of science. One legend claims the doctor's experiment escaped BARC and took up residence in the surrounding woods, while another says the Goatman is actually the ill-fated doctor himself, mutated and insane.

Some websites list the doctor's identity as Dr. Stephen Fletcher, often citing GoatmanHollow.com as their source. Goatman Hollow was a popular haunted attraction in Riverdale, Maryland. The attraction was theatrical in nature and offered an elaborately written, interactive origin story for the monster. The attraction was so popular it was featured on the Travel Channel TV show, *America's Scariest Haunted Attactions 2* in 2007. The attraction's website is comprised of obviously Photoshopped sepia photographs of Fletcher and his family, and a fictitious history of alleged sightings and gruesome, unsolved murders. Goatman Hollow is a prime example of how well-intentioned fiction can influence the real-world legends it's based upon.

While the BARC legend has certain unmistakable B-movie qualities, one shouldn't solely blame the Ed Woods and Roger Cormans of the world. Even the most uninitiated researcher can quickly see why locals would credit BARC for creating a dog-beheading menace like Goaty. A brief glance at the "USDA History Exhibit" on the USDA website lists several examples of new breeds of livestock that were developed there, whatever that means. In the 1920s, BARC created the "meat-type hog" which develops more pork with less feed, as well as several strains of chicken that lay bigger, better-shaped eggs. In the 1930s BARC created a new breed of smaller, meatier turkey named the Beltsville Small White Turkey, which the site boasts is "part of the pedigree of nearly every turkey sold in the US today." Another turkey-based breakthrough was made at Beltsville in the 1950s. BARC scientists discovered the "spontaneous occurrence of parthenogenesis" in turkeys. That is to say, BARC scientists found that certain female turkeys could reproduce without ever coming into contact with a male—the only warm-blooded animal that can do this. The center then developed a strain of Beltsville Whites that could do this at a higher rate. Stories such as this can quickly conjure up daydreams of the campus's various failed experiments, especially if you're like me and read too many comic books. I'd be remiss if I didn't point out that BARC has made lots of helpful innovations that aren't borderline creepy, such as preventing hog cholera, and eradicating glanders disease, two livestock illnesses communicable to humans.

While the BARC campus is the most well-known birthplace of the Goatman, the sprawling, abandoned Glenn Dale Hospital campus is also often blamed for creating the Goatman. The campus consists of twenty-three buildings on approximately two hundred acres of land. The old hospital is located between Fletchertown and Lottsford Roads, the Goatman's two favorite hangouts. While erroneously listed as a former mental hospital or insane asylum in many popular sources, Glenn Dale was actually a tuberculosis sanatorium and isolation hospital. Most versions of the hospital legend involve experimental medical procedures gone awry, resulting in a mutilated and disfigured patient who was either already insane or made so by his tragic metamorphosis. The end result is always an escaped, goatlike lunatic trying to hack up unsuspecting teenagers with an ax.

Just like in Wisconsin, these legends did more to attract youths to these out-of-the-way places than to deter them. Prince George's teen population was, and still is, more than willing to seek out this horror. Searching for the Goatman is a rite of passage in Prince George's. How better for a youngster to prove his or her bravery to his or her peers than by fearlessly driving into the domain of a creature that resembles the devil himself?

As of 2013, the Goatman is associated with a gaggle of locations around Prince George's County, including Governor's Bridge, which crosses the Patuxent River on Governor Bridge Road, and a bridge located on Tucker Road near Andrews Air Force Base in Fort Washington. One blog even claims the thing lives in a rundown house behind St. Mark the Evangelist's School in Hyattsville.

Goatman's infamy has even overshadowed older legends such as one once found at old Irongate Bridge. Nicknamed "Crybaby Bridge," Irongate was located on Lottsford Road in Bowie. The original bridge was torn down and replaced in the late 1980s. In the 1950s locals began alleging that a young mother had cast her unwanted baby into the icy river. Since then, the spirit of a crying infant has been rumored to haunt the bridge. The phantom wails that were once attributed to this sad little ghost are now more often described as the shrill bleating of the Goatman.

Two legends that seem to be unique to Tucker Road involve a hermit rather than a goat-man. The first claims a band of cruel teens burned down the old hermit's home and murdered his beloved goats. Driven insane by his loss, he covered himself in the hides of his deceased four-legged friends and now seeks vengeance on any youth who dares drive down Tucker Road. The second claims that some unnamed enemy cursed the hermit with the head of a goat. Now he hides in an old shack near Tucker Bridge. At midnight he wanders out to the bridge and throws rocks at traffic.

Some legends allege Goatman is a demon conjured up by Satanists. It's even been remarked that the devil himself has an affinity for Prince George's. While an accusation like this could never be proven, it is easy to understand why some residents say this. In 1949, an exorcism occurred in the Prince George's County community of Mount Rainier that inspired William Peter Blatty's 1973 classic horror novel, The Exorcist. There were also accusations of black-magic cults at the University of Maryland College Park campus in the 1970s.

Not only is Maryland's monster the most publicized goat-man in America, he's also the best documented. Relatively new goat-man researchers like myself have a wealth of information to draw from and build on, thanks to two particular individuals. In 1970, Dr. Barry Pearson of the University of Maryland began collecting information on the Goatman during his folklore classes. The majority of this collection would become known as the University of Maryland Folklore Archives, while a few reports ended up in the files of the Delmarva Historical and Cultural Society.

This stockpile of research would later be utilized by a second expert on Maryland's Goatman lore, author and researcher Mark Opsasnick. Opsasnick grew up in Prince George's County in the 1970s, and like his peers, spent many an aimless night legend-tripping rural Prince George's County for signs of the Goatman's presence. Since then, Opsasnick has written two meticulously researched and cited books dealing with the unexplained in Maryland, both of which contain a glut of Goatman information.

In Opsasnick's book *The Real Story Behind the Exorcist: A Study of the Haunted Boy and Other True-Life Horror Legends from Around the Nation's Capital*, he unearthed the first-known mention of the Maryland Goatman in newspapers. In the October 27, 1971, edition of *Prince George's County News* the creature is mentioned alongside various ghost stories. Once Goatman had become famous enough to garner attention from the media, it only took two weeks for the creature to return to the *County News*, this time front page and center. The November

10, 1971, edition published the graphic photograph of a mutilated puppy named Ginger. The dog had belonged to Bowie teen April Edwards.

Opsasnick goes on to chronicle the events in detail. On November 3, 1971, April and her friends had become alarmed by peculiar sounds coming from outside the Edwardses' home and had noticed the silhouette of a large creature walking in a nearby field. Shortly after this, the family's new puppy had vanished. A November 30, 1971, *Washington Post* article tells that Ginger's decapitated remains were found near railroad tracks by two of April's cousins, Ray Hayden and Willie Gheen. Not surprisingly, skeptics blamed these railroad tracks, rather than the Goatman, for Ginger's mutilation.

The same article reveals that April's sixteen-year-old relative, Kathy Edwards, and several other girls reportedly saw the Goatman exit a pickup truck it had been seated on top of near Hayden's home and enter the woods. The murder of Ginger and the dramatic sightings made by the Edwards and Hayden families ignited Goatman fever. Police Captain Lawrence Wheeler notes that numerous other Goatman sightings had been reported. The November 24, 1971, *County News* reports that two carloads of teenagers blocked off a stretch of Tucker Road because they believed they'd cornered the strange creature.

In 1994 Opsasnick interviewed John Hayden, younger brother of Ray Hayden. John revealed that he and Willie Gheen had seen Goatman at 8510 Zug Road around twilight during the 1971 monster flap. He described it as a six-foot-tall hairy animal that made a high-pitched squeal as it ran away on two legs.

If the Maryland Goatman became an inspiration for goat-man legends or sightings in other parts of America, it was likely during this period that it happened. Two articles from the *Washington Post* appeared in newspapers around the country. I found "Maryland's Goatman: Illusory" in newspapers as far west as Tucson, Arizona, from December 8, 1971, and I found "Trees Shelter Strange Silence in Forest of Legendary Goatman" way out in Greeley, Colorado, from

April 6, 1972. And these are just two examples from a blind search through digital newspaper archives. Goatman was doubtlessly national news, though perhaps not front-page center.

As is normally the case when an amazing series of encounters such as this occurs, there was no closure. No one ever came forward saying they had misidentified an animal, no cruel pranksters ever took credit for the slaying of Ginger, nor did anyone ever capture an unknown species of animal either alive or dead. In fact, sightings of large, two-legged, hairy animals continued in Prince George's throughout the 1970s, as documented in *The Real Story Behind the Exorcist*. In September, 1976, a poacher claimed he saw a Bigfoot-like animal walk out of the brush twenty yards from him and head deeper into the woods. The next month a woman named Francine Abell witnessed a six-foot-tall gorilla-like creature walk in front of her car on the Highway 198 exit ramp to I-95 South in Laurel. The creature had rounded shoulders, glowing red eyes, and was covered in gray-brown fur. When her car got nearer, the animal stepped over a railing and fled into the woods. In 1977 a man identified only as a NASA engineer was on his way to Goddard Space Flight Center when he allegedly saw a large, hairy animal being chased through the fog by a dog. The animal supposedly stopped, grabbed the dog, and tossed it onto Highway 95 before disappearing into the woods.

And these were just Goatman sightings. Nineteen-seventies Maryland also had several other high-profile monster cases, including 1973's Sykesville Monster in Carroll County, and 1976's Harewood Park Monster in Baltimore County, both of which involved creatures similar in description to those during the 1971 Goatman outbreak in Prince George's County.

By now you've certainly noticed that none of these sightings describe a satyr-like animal. This was not lost on Opsasnick either. Later in *The Real Story Behind the Exorcist*, he attributes the birth of the Goatman legend to another outbreak of hairy-biped sightings that had occurred decades earlier.

On the night of August 1, 1957, Mr. and Mrs. Reverty Garner of Upper Marlboro drove down lonely, isolated Brown Station Road—roughly fifteen miles south of Fletchertown Road—toward their home tucked away deep within the rural Maryland countryside. Little did they know they were about to experience something absolutely fantastic. As the twenty-something-year-old couple drove into their driveway, a large animal crossed in front of them. Mr. Garner was unable to stop in time and struck the creature, which he described as "a gorilla or something." Mr. Garner turned the vehicle's headlights on the creature and saw a pair of "beady red eyes" coming at them.

The next night, his neighbor, Mrs. H. L. Brady, saw a similar creature spying through her bedroom window as she readied herself for bed. Mr. Brady charged out into the night with his shotgun and fired at the animal as it escaped into the darkness. The Bradys were so frightened that they refused to stay in their own home following the incident.

Thus began a weeklong panic during which a strange apelike animal with glowing red eyes was allegedly sighted in excess of two hundred times, and hunting parties led by both big-game hunters and local authorities combed the woods of Prince George's County without ever laying eyes on what the media had dubbed "the Abominable Phantom." These incidents were covered by several important Washington, DC, papers, including the *Daily News*, the *Evening Star*, even the *Post*. Then, on August 8, Mr. and Mrs. Garner told the *Evening Star* that they now believed that the animal they hit was a neighbor's dog. An elderly, deaf Chow from a nearby farm had recently turned up with a bad limp, and this, the Garner's were now certain, was the animal they'd hit on the night of August 1. This could explain the initial sighting, but it hardly explains the rest, especially the Peeping Tom incident at the Brady residence. Chow dogs aren't known for watching women undress. It's much more likely it was a person who Mrs. Brady misidentified as an unknown bipedal creature. Could all two hundred incidents have been a huge cluster of misidentifications,

Peeping Toms, and pranks? Yes, though it seems almost as unlikely to me as running over an ape in rural Maryland. Despite the vast majority of sightings remaining unexplained, all searches for the crimson-eyed gorilla were canceled, and this strange episode in Maryland history ended as quickly as it began, or so everyone thought.

One can postulate with a fair degree of certainty that the idea of an enormous, hairy, apelike animal with burning red eyes peering through bedroom windows is not something easily forgotten by a small rural community—especially by any youngster who overheard his or her parents discussing the madness that gripped the area. While the Abominable Phantom was never described as having any goatlike characteristics, Opsasnick hypothesizes that the incidents of the summer of 1957 are the birth of a creature that, in less than two decades, proudly menaced the imaginations of Prince George's County.

Opsasnick spoke with descendants of the Brown and Fletcher families, which Fletchertown Road and Brown Station Road are named for. Members of these families believe it was their ancestors who used the Abominable Phantom hysteria as an inspiration for scaring their children into behaving. Over the years, it's believed, these families used the goats they raised as the basis for this bogeyman rather than some exotic ape and dubbed it Goatman. Opsasnick believes that this familial fiend eventually squirmed its way into the imaginations of the general population through schoolyard retellings and ultimately became the phenomenon that it is today.

Again, while Bigfoot and other hairy-biped-like creatures have not been proven to exist, Opsasnick has amassed an impressive collection of sightings. In his book *The Maryland Bigfoot Digest*, Opsasnick has compiled more than three hundred sightings of creatures resembling Bigfoot. Almost fifty of these sightings are either considered Goatman sightings, or at least occurred near Goaty's usual base of operations. The book's earliest possible Goatman/hairy-biped sighting dates back to the seventeenth century. Captain John Smith wrote about an "evil spirit" named Okee worshipped by 1600s Piscataway Indians. He described Okee as a shape-shifter, and said that the Piscataway would paint its devil-like image on their chests. Opsasnick notes that some drawings and wood carvings of Okee resemble modern-day depictions of Bigfoot.

Okee is mentioned numerous times in the EncyclopediaVirginia.org's article "Religion in Early Virginia Indian Society" in regard to the Powhatan Indians. While Okee is sometimes depicted as an ugly creature, he is just as often depicted as a young hunter. The sometimes fearsome interpretations of Okee were often associated with Satan by seventeenth-century Christians. There seems to be a duality between the two extremely different depictions of Okee. An ugly version of Okee is generally thought to have power over war and the afterlife, whereas the handsome creature lorded over the animals. It is noteworthy that the article states that the Powhatans would wear antlers during certain Okee ceremonies. If the Piscataway had similar ceremonies, this could explain the devil-like creature painted on their chests. If a clear connection could ever be made between Okee and the Goatman, it would without a doubt make Maryland the birthplace of Goatman, but the chances of that ever happening are unlikely indeed.

While the Maryland Goatman will probably never be proven to predate European colonization, *The Maryland Bigfoot Digest* has collected reports of strange Bigfoot-like creatures in the woods of Prince George's County dating back to the 1920s, and the oldest mention of the Goatman by name in the University of Maryland Folklore Archives that I'm aware of refers to an incident in 1967. Not a bad pedigree, for sure.

However, much like in Wisconsin, one sighting does describe an actual goat-man. Matt Lake's book *Weird Maryland* includes an encounter reported by someone identified only as "TheStereoGod," likely an Internet screen name. The incident happened to his friend's oldest daughter near off-base military housing in the Prince George's city of Summerfield, and was related to him secondhand. The girls had gone off to play at a nearby creek before dinner. When they were called in to dinner, only the youngest returned. When he went to retrieve the other girl, he found her huddled and crying, pointing at the other side of the creek. It wasn't until they returned home that she stopped sobbing. She told him that after being left alone she'd noticed something that appeared to be a goat near the water, but it soon stood up on two legs and walked into the woods. When their father investigated, hoofprints were found. Later that night, Dad first learned of the Maryland Goatman legend via the Internet.

Theories abound regarding the Maryland monster's genesis, but for every teen who claims his cousin's roommate's nephew knows a guy who read top-secret classified papers about the Goatman at BARC, or for every Bigfoot researcher who thinks the Goatman was inspired by a hairy-biped sighting, there are skeptics who have their own theories. One such fellow is Father Joseph Jenkins, a pastor at Holy Family Church in Mitchellville. In April, 1998, Jenkins published a piece called "The Goatman of Prince George's County" on his personal blog. After reminiscing about how the Goatman functioned as a sort of bogeyman during his childhood in the 1960s and 1970s, he started his own inquiry. Jenkins spoke with many senior parishioners in Prince George's County, particularly at St. Mary's of the Assumption in Upper Marlboro. Jenkins then listed several eccentrics who could have inspired the legend. The foremost possible culprit could have been a man named Dominic. Dominic was a trapper who would wander the waterways through the then heavily wooded areas of Upper Marlboro from spring until autumn hunting turtles. He dressed in fur and carried a walking stick and whatever tools he'd need to get through the season—maybe even a hatchet or ax? Dominic was usually covered in mud from sticking his arms into the banks of creeks and generally looked unkempt. Late in his life, when more and more land became privately owned, he'd have to wander the roadways on foot to get from place to place. Jenkins believes that it's along these roads that teens would have likely seen him and perhaps started spreading stories about him. The blog goes on to mention a Joe C. and a George T. who were contemporaries of Dominic and lived similar lifestyles. Jenkins also mentions that one senior he interviewed recalled a peculiar character who could have been inspired by any of the three—a hermit who always wore a long fur coat regardless of weather or temperature. He was known as "the Coatman," which could have been corrupted to "Goatman" after multiple retellings.

A second, much more damaging blow to Goatman's validity also came in 1998, at a time when the monster was experiencing a renaissance. The Goatman had just got done hobnobbing with Mulder and Scully in the comic book adaptation of *the X-Files*, and starring on the Discovery Channel program *Into the Unknown*. It was this cable-television debut that inspired *Washington City Paper* reporter Sean Daly to write an odd but fascinating piece of Gonzo journalism with the wordy title "The Legend of Goatman: P.G. County's Ax-Wielding, Dog-Beheading and Much Loved Urban Legend Makes a 90's Comeback." In this article, Daly met up with Mark Opsasnick and tooled around Prince George's County reliving the Goatman hysteria of the 1970s.

While visiting the train tracks where the Edwards family's dead pup was found, Opsasnick and Daly had a chance encounter with then forty-eight-year-old Ray Hayden, one of the boys who'd found Ginger. Ray is also the older brother of John, one of the boys who allegedly saw Goatman in 1971. When asked about the 1971 Goatman outbreak, the foul-mouthed Ray alleged that Ginger was merely hit by a train and that John Hayden and Willie Gheen had made up Goatman's involvement to frighten neighbors. Ray continued with the revelation that Goatman was really just a filthy but friendly wino named either Albert Abel or Albert Thompson. Albert allegedly walked the train tracks with a double-edged ax—a story Ray stuck with during a 1999 interview on Animal Planet's TV show *Animal X*. When pressed for additional information, Ray instructed the two investigators to visit

Goatman: Flesh or Folklore?

Ascension Catholic Church cemetery on Zug Road; there, Ray assured them, they'd find the Goatman. Opsasnick and Daly spent the remainder of the evening searching the cemetery, but never found the Goatman. If "Albert" was buried there, he must've been relegated to an unmarked grave. Daly attempted to interview John Hayden later, but he was busy with work and seemed hostile about the subject. When Daly mentioned Ray's accusation, John became visibly agitated and pointed out that Ray wasn't present when he and Gheen had their encounter with the strange animal. Was the 1971 incident that made Goatman a household name in Prince George's just a prank by John Hayden and Gheen? Was the Abominable Phantom of the 1950s really just an elderly dog? Even If the answer is yes to both questions, that only explains a handful of the roughly three hundred hairy-biped sightings in Opsasnick's *Maryland Bigfoot Digest*.

Nowadays the Goatman's original domain—the area around Lottfsford and Fletchertown Roads—would be unrecognizable to anyone who'd been away since 1970s Goatman Mania. The thick, ominous woods interrupted occasionally by a ramshackle shanty is now modern housing developments. If Goatman really is some sort of wild animal—mutated or otherwise—he's quickly running out of places to hide in Prince George's. But sightings of Bigfoot-like creatures continue in the Free State. In August of 2000, the Baltimore ABC affiliate reported that construction workers were chased from a Hanover, Maryland, construction site by a twelve-foot-tall hairy creature that left fifteen-inch-long footprints. Baltimore media labeled the animal Bigfoot, but if you mention the sighting eighteen miles to the north in Prince George's, they'll tell you it was probably Goatman. But despite a loss of habitat and a growing number of Chow dogs, transients, trappers, and possible pranksters who have threatened to destroy his legend, the Goatman has endured.

The late Mark Chorvinsky was also interviewed in Daly's 1998 article. Chorvinsky was a Goatman aficionado as well as editor/publisher of *Strange Magazine*. I think he summed it up best: "People love campfire tales…Twenty years from now, people will still be talking about Goatman. Even more so than today." As I write this, there are still four years left before I can call Chorvinsky a prophet, and the monster's notoriety continues to grow. In 2010 the mockumentary horror film *Jimmy Tupper vs. the Goatman of Bowie* debuted at the South By Southwest film festival in Austin. In 2012 the low-budget gore fest *Deadly Detour: The Goatman Murders* went straight to DVD.

While researching this book, Barbara of Bowie, Maryland, wrote me in November, 2013. "We who have lived in Bowie most of our lives know all about the Goatman. [Is he just] folklore? I doubt it. He has been seen and heard late at night when the moon is full, and the remnants of his meals [are] found scattered throughout the woods along Highbridge [Road] and other back roads here and there. His eyes are yellow, and he walks on two legs at times. Oh yes, little children fear him. Bigger kids worship him [because they] fear that a lack of respect will bring the wrath of the Goatman down on them! Boo!"

I believe Chorvinsky was correct.

CHAPTER 5
FISHY MAN-GOAT OF LAKE WORTH

If Maryland's Goatman mania of the 1970s really did seed some American imaginations via either nationally syndicated Washington Post articles or word of mouth, the possible existence of such a creature was already old news to the people of Fort Worth, Texas. The Lake Worth Monster made its debut more than a year before the *Prince George's County News* first printed the name Goatman.

An article by Jim Marrs entitled "Fishy Man-Goat Terrifies Couples Parked at Lake Worth"—complete with ridicule hidden in the headline—was published in the July 10, 1969, edition of the *Fort Worth Star-Telegram*. Shortly after midnight on the morning of July 10, Mr. and Mrs. John Reichart were parked at Lake Worth with two other couples when they encountered a savage creature that would become known as the Lake Worth Monster, also known as Goatman. A large, hairy animal described as a cross between a human and a goat with what was most peculiar of all—scales—leaped out of the treetops and onto the hood of their car. John Reichart told the police that the beast tried to grab his wife through the car window, but he and the others were able to speed away to the nearest police station and report the incident. The Reicharts pointed out an eighteen-inch-long scratch down the side of their car, which they suspected had been made by the creature's claws. In the same article, the police admitted they'd been receiving complaints about a strange creature at Lake Worth over the previous two months, but had written it off as crank calls. The incident had frightened the witnesses to such an extent that six police units investigated the scene but found nothing unusual. The article ends with the police blaming the event on a foolhardy prankster. Thus began the summer of the Goatman.

The Lake Worth Monster was sighted again after midnight on July 11 by Jack Harris, who witnessed the creature crossing a road that lead into the Lake Worth Nature Center. Jack had set out to find the creature following the July 10 article, as did many others, apparently. Not long after the creature had crossed the road, about twenty to thirty people who were also looking for the beast gathered and watched as it walked up and down a bluff. When the witnesses tried to approach the animal, it lifted a car tire complete with rim that had been discarded nearby and hurled it some five hundred feet toward the crowd, causing them to scatter. A witness named Ronny Armstrong backed his car into a tree trying to escape. When police arrived, one of the deputies attempted to laugh off the witness testimony, until a strange howl came from the woods and sent the officers retreating to their squad car. The incident was recapped later that day in the *Star-Telegraph* with the headline "Police, Residents Observe but Can't Identify Monster," along with a photograph of Harris and Armstrong inspecting the tire that had been launched at the crowd. Various witnesses agreed the creature weighed around three hundred pounds, walked on two legs, and was covered in whitish-gray fur. Harris described its howl as "pitiful," as if it were in pain. In the article, police suspected the creature to be a person wearing an ape suit, while Fort Worth Museum of Science and History spokesperson

Goatman: Flesh or Folklore?

Helmuth Naumer and Lake Worth Park naturalist Dick Prall blamed the panic on a pet bobcat that was known to have been turned loose in the park. The cat was fond of people, and had been known to scare park patrons by leaping from tree branches onto cars. While the bobcat theory seems to mesh somewhat with the initial sighting on July 10, one would be hard pressed to confuse a bobcat with a scaly goatman, even in the grip of panic.

On July 14, the *Star-Telegram* published a piece called "Ghosts Seen on Greer Island," implying a possible otherworldly connection. A man named Mike Kinson reported that in addition to having witnessed misty apparitions at Lake Worth, he'd also seen the Lake Worth Monster

Following the initial recorded sightings, unsanctioned search parties and rag-tag groups of hunters regularly combed the area for weeks, usually armed with hunting rifles. Tracks were found allegedly measuring sixteen inches long by eight inches wide at the toes. Jim Stephens of Bluemound claimed the beast leaped onto his moving car, causing him and his passengers to collide with a tree. Only then did the animal release his grip on the car and escape into the woods. Sheep with broken necks were found by Mr. and Mrs. James Bramble, who attributed the sheep's deaths to the beast. They heard the monster's cry and smelled its horrible odor, but never saw the thing. One hunter reportedly shot the animal and followed a trail of blood that disappeared into Lake Worth, causing many to suspect the creature lived on Greer Island.

A local dress-shop owner named Allen Plaster became the only person to take a photo of the monster; in fact, it's the only known photograph ever taken of any alleged goat-man. The photograph is a blurry, close-range photograph of a large, white Bigfoot-like animal, standing at profile, with a broad body and a relatively small head. Plaster was interviewed in the June 8, 2006, *Star-Telegraph* article "1969 Lake Worth Monster, Was the "Goat-Man" Hulk or Hoax?" Plaster and some of his friends had made it a habit to go out two or three times a week in search of the Goatman. Plaster was driving along the lakeshore one night with a friend identified only as Kay, when she shouted she could see the infamous beast. Plaster says the animal stood up from a three-foot-high patch of weeds. Plaster stopped the car and snapped a Polaroid instant picture of the creature as it ran away. In hindsight, Plaster now believes the image isn't photographic proof of a monster, but merely a prankster. Upon reflection, he believes the supposed creature was waiting there to be seen. As of 2013, scans of the photo are readily available all over the Internet, but Plaster gave his only copy to local private investigator and author Sallie Ann Clarke, who wrote the self-published book *The Lake Worth Monster of Greer Island, Fort Worth, Texas*, which was a semifictitious book that approached the situation with a good deal of levity.

The August 8, 2009, *NBC-5 Dallas–Fort Worth* article, "Mystery Still Engulfs Lake Worth Monster" featured quotes from eighty-year-old Richard Lederer, Clarke's husband. At the time, Ms. Clarke was unavailable for comment, as her health and memory were in decline due to a series of strokes. Lederer stated his wife always regretted that she didn't write the book as pure unembellished history, as she herself witnessed the Lake Worth Monster on three occasions after she published her book.

While Clarke's book is of little use to researchers given its less-than-honest chronicling of the Lake Worth Monster scare, it did reveal that prior to the summer of 1969, some local youths had been frequenting the Lake Worth area in search of a creature called "the Mud Monster," which could likely have been the monster police had received reports of prior to the Reichart attack on July 10.

To put an end to the controversy, Sallie Ann Clarke once offered a reward of several thousand dollars to anyone who could pass a polygraph test proving they were the Lake Worth Monster, but no one so much as offered to take the test.

Several people have since come forward or been implicated as Lake Worth Monster pranksters. Jim Marrs, the reporter who broke the story for the *Star-Telegraph*, told newspapers in 1989 that police had questioned a group of high school students in 1969 who had been caught with a headless gorilla costume and mask, though this was never reported in any newspaper of the day, and no police report has been found to substantiate the claim.

An anonymous, hand-written letter was sent to a *Star-Telegraph* reporter in 2005 claiming that the letter's author and a fellow North Side High School student would go out to the lake and scare motorists with a gorilla suit and a homemade tinfoil mask—which I suppose could resemble fish scales to a frightened person. The writer states that the reason he and his friend hoaxed the Reicharts and company that fateful night was because they'd always heard stories about "monsters and creatures that would attack parkers."

A man identified only as Vinzens took credit for the tire-throwing incident in the August 2009 edition of *Fort Worth, Texas Magazine.* He claimed the tire only went airborne because it struck a rock as it rolled down the hill.

A kennel owner recently came forward admitting he'd lost a Japanese macaque monkey that summer and suspected that it could have been responsible for the sightings, though this is just as unsatisfactory as the bobcat explanation. While a macaque's light-colored fur matches some descriptions given of the Lake Worth Monster, macaques only weigh between nineteen and twenty-five pounds, and normally stand roughly two feet in height. Also, if this kennel owner knew an exotic animal like a macaque was loose at Lake Worth during a monster scare, one certainly wonders why he waited so many years to mention it to the media instead of doing so at the height of monster fever.

The last known sighting during this spate can be found in Loren Coleman's book, *Mysterious America,* via a Bigfoot researcher named John Green. A man named Charles Buchanan was asleep in a sleeping bag in the back of his pickup truck at Lake Worth on November 7, 1969. Buchanan was awakened in the middle of the night when the creature tried lifting him into the air. In his panic, Buchanan was able to give the thing a bag of leftover chicken that was lying nearby. Satisfied, the monster then swam away toward Greer Island.

The only rational explanation for the whole ordeal is that it was some peculiar combination of a misidentified animal and the work of multiple pranksters or liars—but there's as much hard evidence to support that theory as there is that a goat-man was roaming around Lake Worth in 1969.

The Lake Worth Monster's infamy is so great that strange creature sightings hundreds of miles away are attributed to him. In 2013, the Destination America television show *Monsters and Mysteries in America* featured a half-hour segment on the Lake Worth Monster. After the furor of 1969 had been retold, the show featured a so-called Lake Worth Monster encounter from Mount Nebo, Texas, a rural area outside of San Angelo, some 230 miles southwest of Lake Worth.

Sometime during the 1990s, a teenager named Doug Sheldon had arranged a nocturnal rendezvous with friends on Mount Nebo, an area where they would often camp or hang out. Instead of his friends, Sheldon saw a terrifying animal that he described as a six-feet-eight-inches tall, furry, manlike creature with small, six- to seven-inch-long horns on its forehead.

Sheldon fled and later found his friends, who insisted they'd yet to visit the meeting place. After a few good laughs at Sheldon's expense, he was able to convince his friends to go look for the monster. When they arrived, they saw the strange thing silhouetted against the moonlight. When it howled, the three teens fled.

People still have the occasional odd experience at Lake Worth, but nothing near the magnitude of the 1969 eruption. Those who believe the Lake Worth Monster was a Bigfoot-like creature theorize that the creature may have died from the gunshot wound it allegedly sustained, or that it was permanently frightened from the area. The research of Texas monster hunters Ken Gerhard and Nick Redfern's disagrees. According to their book, *Monsters of Texas*, the two discovered a "Bigfoot teepee" deep within the woods of Greer Island in 2005. Teepees such as the one found at Lake Worth are peculiar pyramid-like structures made of tree branches that have been ripped or twisted off nearby trees. While the function of these baffling arrangements remains a mystery, they are often found near locations with known hairy-biped activity. Despite this sign of activity, the Lake Worth Monster hasn't been seen in years. Perhaps if Fort Worth does have a fishy goat-man, he learned his lesson and is now avoiding humans at all costs.

Despite a lack of activity at the lake, the monster has become firmly entrenched in Fort Worth pop culture. In 1975, Johnny Simmons created a folk/rock opera called *The Lake Worth Monster*. The plot shifts between the playwright's own personal demons and the antics of the Goatman. The musical was revived again in 1989.

In 2009, the Fort Worth Nature Center and Refuge officially embraced the beast by creating the first annual Lake Worth Monster Bash. The outdoor festival was designed to lure Forth Worth families out into nature, where they could hike to locations where the monster was sighted, visit historic buildings on the refuge, and enjoy local music. The 2010 event featured goat-hair weaving and tire-throwing competitions.

While a rock opera and a festival would be enough to secure any monster's continued existence, it's likely the various summer camps around Lake Worth are what will keep the Goatman alive for generations. No unnerving night around a campfire at Lake Worth is complete without a terrifying retelling of the summer of 1969—with a few ad-libbed stories of children stolen away during the night, of course.

CHAPTER 6

TEXAS'S HOOVED HOARD

The Texas Goatman's presence isn't exclusive to Lake Worth, unlike Maryland's Goatman, which seems to be bound to Prince George's County. Every time I was certain I'd found every Texas locale Goaty was associated with, another would pop up. Given enough time and resources I'm certain a person could find at least one Goatman legend or sighting in each of Texas's 254 counties. The Lake Worth Monster's various assaults were reported in newspapers and in television and radio broadcasts all over Texas. The Lake Worth Monster could easily have inspired many of the state's other Goatman legends.

A legend from neighboring Dallas is especially reminiscent of the 1969 Lake Worth Monster scare. Dallas's creature is said to lurk in the woods around White Rock Lake, located in a state park in the suburbs of northeastern Dallas. Known only as the Goatman, it has horns, a humanlike face, and a sickly green complexion, and it walks upright on two goatlike legs. The Goatman of White Rock Lake is said to enjoy throwing objects at witnesses. The beast is said to wander out of the woods and throw trash—even old tires—at those who visit the lake. One can't help but suspect these stories became accidentally attached to White Rock Lake by confused or misinformed residents who'd heard about the Lake Worth scare.

Lake Worth's monster is basically a celebrity around Fort Worth. With all of the recorded sightings, the book, and a festival named after it, finding information on the monster was relatively easy. The monster had its own folder in the archives of the Fort Worth Library, for goodness' sake. Dallas's version of the critter was much more elusive. The Dallas Historical Society researcher I spoke with seemed oblivious to the creature, and was rather disinterested in the subject to say the least, while the helpful and courteous staff at the Dallas Public Library could only direct me toward a few brief paragraphs in the book *Weird Texas* which claims encounters with the creature occurred in both the 1970s and 1980s. I scoured numerous online newspaper archives for any mention of the Goatman in the Dallas area but found no sightings of the creature. Despite a lack of recorded sightings, Dallas's Goatman is gaining in notoriety. As of 2013, the Dallas-based Lakewood Brewing Company was bottling an Indian Black Lager named Goatman. Each longneck's label carried a warning that Goatman's "a territorial terror who doesn't like anybody loitering in his neck of the woods."

The only sighting of the Goatman of White Rock Lake I've found documented comes from goat-man aficionado Nick Redfern. Nick has authored various books, including *Three Men Seeking Monsters*, and is a regular contributor at Cryptomundo.com. Redfern's Mania.com article "Coming of the Goatman" recounts a mid-August 2001 encounter as reported to him by an eyewitness named Sandy Grace. Grace was jogging on a trail that meandered around White Rock Lake. At around two o'clock in the afternoon, a large, menacing, grinning, horned creature covered in coarse brown hair approached her from the woods. When it got a dozen or so feet from her, there was a blinding flash of light, and the entity vanished. Grace noted that before she noticed the creature she was overcome by what she could only describe as a panic attack, something that she had never before personally experienced. This supernaturally laced encounter and the mention of a panic attack led Redfern to discuss goatlike figures from mythology, including satyrs and Pan.

While Grace's 2001 Dallas sighting is bizarre indeed, given its paranormal quality when compared to the more relatively mundane sightings in the city of Fort Worth, the majority of Texas's Goatman legends wander into the realm of the paranormal. This is in contrast with the Maryland legends, the majority of which have a science-run-amok quality. In McLennan County, a genetically engineered goat-man is said to live under a railroad trestle in the city of West, but almost all of Texas's other goat-man legends are much more supernatural in nature. For instance, McLennan's other goat-man is a reanimated mutant that devours children and teens in Cameron Park and along the banks of Lake Waco, and the Bosque and Brazos Rivers in Waco. The creature's father believed his deformed child to be an ungodly abomination and killed it with an ax. The child's grave was later found empty. His close resemblance to the devil is said to be what kept him from entering heaven. Oh, and that's just a small sample when it comes to the fantastic tales surrounding the Texas goat-men.

In Burkburnett in Wichita County, a bridge crossing Gilbert's Creek near Sheppard Air Force Base is reputed to be haunted by the ghost of a man with a goat's lower half. His presence is blamed on a satanic church that once operated or presently operates near the bridge. In Johnson County, a demonic goat-man named Old Foamy resides at a shailow water crossing on Old Foamy Road in Cleburne. The beast is blamed for several alleged hangings and dismemberments, and also enjoys leaping onto cars and throwing dead animals at motorists. Old Foamy can be summoned by parking at the crossing and honking a car horn three times. Though be warned—the only way to send the creature back is by driving in reverse and honking thrice more. The Hills County Goatman hangs out in "Goatman's Tunnel," in Files Valley. The haunted tunnel comes complete with bleeding walls. In Hamilton the Goatman lives in a drainage pipe on Pecan Creek Trail and peeks around corners at people foolish enough to crawl inside. In Wylie, he appears on the hood of your car and dances a jig.

Bell County has numerous Goatman stories. At Fort Hood he leaps out of the woods and chases cars. Should someone be brave enough to chase the beast down, he retreats onto restricted land. Though this legend seems to imply the Goatman could be some escaped army experiment, the rest of Bell County's Goatman legends maintain the otherworldly theme. In Temple, a sulfuric-smelling Goatman supposedly lurks along the Tenth Street railroad tracks looking for children who stray too near the rails. In Belton he prowls along Lake Belton striking from the murky waters at night to steal away anyone wandering alone near the shore. Often his presence is announced via a vision of a burning crucifix in the distance. Meanwhile, just south of the city of Belton, he's said to reside on Camp Tahuaya land, and is a favorite campfire ghoul for Boy Scout troops. The Tahuaya Goatman is said to live in a cave that's barely big enough for two Webelos to navigate shoulder to shoulder.

Navarro County's Goatman in Emhouse is known to terrorize parked lovers, and occasionally raid suburban bird feeders. Channelview's Van Road is rumored to have been the scene of satanic sacrifices that birthed a Goatman that chases nocturnal motorists in fits of bloodlust. Out by the Gulf Coast, Goatman lives in an abandoned house on Goatman's Road in Baytown. The creature's described as a hairy, seven-foot-tall humanoid with horns, hooves, and a bald head covered in warts—yuck. In Colorado County in Matthews, he's strong enough to stop cars with his bare hands and is even known to show up at your front door demanding food!

While it seems probable that the Lake Worth Monster instigated Goatman's proliferation across Texas, there is a second monster that could have inspired such terrifying tales, not only in Texas, but across the entire country. But unlike the Goatman, this monster's validity has never been questioned.

The incidents that follow are summarized from Joseph Geringer's CrimeLibrary.com article "The Phantom Killer: Texarkana Moonlight Murders." In the early-morning hours of February 22, 1946, Jimmy Hollis and Mary Jeanne Larey parked on a secluded road outside of Texarkana, which was known unofficially as Lovers' Lane. Roughly ten minutes after arriving they were interrupted by a tap on the window, and the inside of the vehicle was illuminated by a flashlight's beam. Thinking it was a policeman, the two exited the car, only to find it was a man wearing a homemade burlap mask, holding a handgun. The masked man ordered Hollis to remove his pants. When Hollis did, the stranger hit him over the head with the gun, cracking his skull. He then chased Larey down the road and tackled her to the ground. The fiend then began molesting her, but was interrupted by distant headlights. Before fleeing, he beat her.

On March 24 of that year, a passing motorist discovered the bodies of Richard L. Griffin and Polly Ann Moore inside Griffin's 1941 Oldsmobile. Both had been shot in the head. Police discovered that Polly had been sexually assaulted and killed outside the car before being dragged back into the vehicle.

On April 14, the bodies of two teenagers, Paul Martin and Betty Jo Booker, were found. Both had been shot multiple times, and Booker had been sexually assaulted. The assailant had attacked three times and taken four victims in just three months. The media needed a name for the killer. He was dubbed "the Phantom," because of his ability to elude capture. Finally on the night of May 3, the Phantom struck one last time. As Virgil Stark sat in a recliner reading a newspaper in his rural farmhouse, the Phantom fired a shot through the parlor window, hitting him in the head and killing him instantly. Virgil's wife, Katy, ran downstairs, and upon finding the body, attempted to dial the police. She was shot in the head twice, but miraculously survived. She ran to the road and was picked up by a passing car and taken to a nearby hospital.

Goatman: Flesh or Folklore?

The slayings became known as the "Moonlight Murders." The killing spree was headline news all over the country, even gaining coverage internationally via the London Times. These killings were the first of their kind in America: a sexually motivated killer preying on young couples—all but one of which were likely about to engage in intimacy in a parked vehicle. Though law enforcement officials investigated several suspects, no one was ever convicted of the crime. The Phantom, though easily now in his eighties, could still be wandering the streets of some small town even today. He could be that disarmingly pleasant old man who sits across from you at church, his deviant past hidden behind dentures and a smile. Perhaps if the Phantom had been apprehended, the story would have become nothing more than a dark chapter in history.

The November 8, 1960, edition of the syndicated advice column "Dear Abby" featured a correspondence from a girl named Jeanette, relating a potentially true story she'd heard from a friend about an escaped convict with a hook for a hand who preyed on parked teenagers. While this is the first known appearance of "Hook Man" in print, folklorists across America and Canada had been collecting variations of the tale from their students since the 1950s. The validity of the story didn't matter to Jeanette. She wrote that regardless of its legitimacy, the story had frightened her so that she'd never park to make out as long as she lived. She also hoped her letter would persuade other girls in the same manner.

It's believed that the Phantom's handiwork spawned these urban legends that still haunt the youths of today. Given the horrific nature of the Phantom's murders, it's possible that—through constant retelling—the Phantom became a hook-handed lunatic in cautionary tales whispered in high school hallways. However, how did either the Phantom or the Hook Man take on the characteristics of a man-goat? An important piece of the puzzle is missing, and until I find that piece, I'm not willing to proclaim Texarkana the unwitting birthplace of the Goatman, if for no other reason than respect for the Phantom's victims.

CHAPTER 7

THE GHOST AT GOATMAN'S BRIDGE

Though Texas boasts a plethora of supernatural goat-men, one in particular deserves a bit more attention than the rest. Forty miles to the north of Lake Worth is the city of Denton, a city whose most famous resident is a ghost—Goatman's ghost, of course. This specter is said to haunt Old Alton Bridge—named after Denton County's long-vanished former county seat. More popularly known as Goatman's Bridge, this 140-foot-long iron-through-truss bridge sits thirty feet above Hickory Creek. The bridge was installed in 1884 over an old cattle crossing to connect Denton to Lewisville via the old postal road and Ranger's trail. Originally built to accommodate horses-drawn wagons, the bridge is extremely narrow. Whenever automobiles would attempt to cross at night, drivers would have to stop and sound their horn to alert oncoming traffic that they were crossing.

There are nearly as many variations to the legend of Goatman's Bridge as all the other Texas goat-man legends combined. Some versions say a goat farmer and his herd were run off the side of the

Goatman: Flesh or Folklore?

bridge by drunken cowboys and drowned, dooming the farmer and his herd to haunt the bridge for all eternity. Other versions say the creature was accidentally summoned to our world by satanic worship—a claim reiterated all over the country. Most versions, though, involve a lynching, and most Internet sources claim the poor soul hanged was named Oscar Washburn, an event usually said to have taken place in 1938.

According to legend, Oscar was an African-American goat farmer who moved his family into a house near Hickory Creek. Oscar proved popular in the community of Denton, too popular for a black man in Jim Crow–era Texas. One night, just before dawn, after the moon had set and the night was dark, a group of Ku Klux Klansmen quietly drove across Old Alton Bridge, their headlights off to avoid detection. The hateful thugs burst into the Washburn home and dragged Oscar into the night. There, in the pitch-black Denton night, they tied a noose around his neck and hanged him over the side of Old Alton Bridge. As the savage Klansmen reveled in Washburn's death, they heard a loud splash. When they looked over the side of the bridge, Oscar's body was gone. Some versions of the legend say the man's head was removed by the tension of the noose, while others say Washburn's body simply vanished into thin air. All versions agree the cruel men who hanged him returned to the Washburn home and murdered his family. Soon after, a half-man, half-goat creature was said to stalk the woods around the bridge. Some stories say that Washburn's spirit returned looking for his missing head, and when he didn't find it, wrenched the head off one of his own goats and used it instead.

There are several dares that have become attached to Goatman's Bridge over the years, and they've become a favorite pastime for some of the community's younger citizenry, especially around Halloween. The dares include but aren't limited to driving across the bridge with your headlights off, or parking on the bridge on Halloween night with your car's headlights off and honking the horn twice. Both will supposedly result in seeing the glowing red eyes of the Goatman peering at you from the far end of the bridge. Unfortunately for thrill seekers, neither dare is possible these days, as the bridge has been closed to vehicles since around 2001. Despite this, adventurous kids still visit the bridge on foot.

The majority of the Denton legends also blame the Goatman for an abundance of abandoned cars found near the bridge, the motorists never found. Numerous Internet websites claim the disappearances began on the unusually specific date of November 16, 1967, and that the events were well documented in Denton's newspaper.

Unlike in the Fort Worth or Dallas areas, there doesn't seem to be any recorded sightings of a physical creature, so I sifted through countless digital scans of the *Denton Record-Chronicle* to see if I could prove or disprove any of the names, events, or dates associated with the Goatman's Bridge legends.

The Ku Klux Klan's presence in the legend isn't surprising. The Klan was a menace in Denton as it was throughout the rest of the southern United States for a regrettably long time. I found few mentions of their presence in the *Record-Chronicle*, but their antics are recorded elsewhere. The Klan marched and rode through Denton several times in the 1920s, as pointed out in the article "The Quakertown Story" from the winter 1991 issue of *The Denton Review*. To make a long story short, the KKK were unhappy the black community of Quakertown was located so near the all-white, all-female College of Industrial Arts, though if a KKK-incited lynching occurred in Denton, I've not been able to verify it.

Much to my surprise, though, Oscar Washburn was a real person living in Denton, and he was murdered. According to an article called "Bond Not Yet Fixed for Alleged Slayer of Brother-In-Law" in the October 17, 1917, *Record-Chronicle*, Oscar Washburn was shot once through the heart by O. T. "Iron" Miller, and died instantly. Miller, who was living in the Washburn residence, claimed Washburn had whipped his sister, though seventeen-year-old Mrs. Washburn said she'd only been slapped—as if that's much of a difference. Miller turned himself in to authorities. The article states that Washburn and his family had been living on the property of a Mr. J. M. Sanders in the town of Aubrey for the past ten or twelve years—roughly twenty miles from Old Alton Bridge—and that Washburn left behind three young children he'd sired with a former wife. I could not find any mention of an occupation, though I suspect farmwork. I have no theory as to how Washburn became associated with an alleged lynching at Old Alton Bridge in the 1930s. The only other mention of the Washburn murder I could find in newspapers was in the April 7, 1919, *Galveston Daily News*. The one-paragraph story, "Gets Five-Year Suspended Sentence on Murder Charge," says that Miller was found guilty of manslaughter.

Emboldened by my discoveries, I began looking into the alleged abandoned-cars and missing-persons reports. I found no mention of people or an abandoned car vanishing mysteriously on November 16, 1967. I did, however, find a report of a missing car being recovered west of Old Alton Bridge in the January 11, 1967, *Record-Chronicle*. The car was reported missing by Robert Carroll Golden of Irving on January 8. The car was found the next day with several hundred dollars of equipment stripped from it. A similar incident was reported in the October 29, 1973, *Record-Chronicle*. A stolen 1973 Pontiac was found burned near Old Alton Bridge. Two other vehicles had been stolen as well, with a fourteen-year-old arrested in Dallas when he was found sitting in one of the vehicles.

There were two missing-persons cases that ended gruesomely in 1966 and 1967, though both occurred in or just outside of Fort Worth, nowhere near Old Alton Bridge. Both incidents were pulled from the Associated Press and published in the *Record-Chronicle*. The August 9, 1966, edition's front page was headlined with "Search Party Locates Body of Missing Girl." A fisherman discovered an abandoned car outside of Fort Worth. When he opened the trunk, he found the bodies of seventeen-year-old Robert Brand and his cousin, sixteen-year-old

Jack Dunnam. Sixteen-year-old Edna Louise Sullivan, whose name was "scrawled across the window of the death car," was found dead in a field twelve miles south of Fort Worth by a search party lead by one of two murder suspects, eighteen-year-old Roy Green. According to an emotional statement given by Green to lawmen and the press, he and twenty-year-old Kenneth McDuff, both of Marlin, Texas, allegedly drove to Fort Worth with the intention of a "sexual escapade with a parked couple." They ran across the three teenagers, and ordered the boys into the trunk of their own car and the girl into McDuff and Green's trunk. The boys were driven to a field by McDuff, where they were shot and killed. According to Green, the two then took Sullivan to a different field, where she was raped three times before being killed. Both McDuff and Green were in custody at the time of the article. McDuff denied any knowledge of or involvement with the murders.

The February 5, 1967, edition ran the story "Woman Found Raped, Killed Near Trinity." Thirty-seven-year-old housewife Mildred May's body was found on a river levy in east Fort Worth. She had been raped and strangled with such strength that her neck had been broken. She was then thrown from a car. Her husband returned home from work and found her missing, then called police. The body was discovered by two teenagers riding a motor scooter.

Eventually, I did discover a death that occurred near Old Alton Bridge. The front page of the October 3, 1977, *Record-Chronicle* reads "Search Team Finds Woman's Body." A child named Suzie Mages had gone missing seven days earlier at a Burger King in a Denton shopping mall. As police and members of the girl's family combed Denton, a search party stumbled across the body of a twenty-five-year-old Dallas woman down by Hickory Creek. The woman was wearing a nightgown and was "doubled over" on a blue plaid blanket. A teddy bear, some clothes, and an empty prescription for barbiturates were found with the body. The woman's body had been there for perhaps two days. They found her vehicle in a pasture just west of the bridge.

Goatman: Flesh or Folklore?

The woman's death, seemingly a suicide, was thought to be unrelated to the Mages disappearance.

Stories like these—even the two Fort Worth murders—obviously would have left an impression on any reader of the *Record-Chronicle*. These types of stories, along with others like them, were certainly discussed within the community, and would have been overheard by impressionable young ears. One can see how events such as these, coupled with with police finding the husks of burned cars near Old Alton Bridge could create legends. While I couldn't determine exactly when stories about Old Alton Bridge being haunted first began, it was likely early in the structure's existence. An 1870s shoot-out between lawmen and the infamous Sam Bass Gang that occurred at Hickory Creek prior to the construction of Old Alton Bridge is said to be a cause of paranormal activity at the bridge. There is also a Crybaby Bridge legend there as well. Both of these legends are independent of the Goatman stories.

A different version of the lynching story says the Goatman was lynched at Old Alton Bridge after murdering his entire family, and just like in other versions, he was accidentally beheaded, and his spirit used the head of one of his goats. The inspiration for this story is likely a Cooke County man named John Quincy Adams Crews. According to an undated newspaper clipping I received from a Fort Worth resident, Crews had gotten into an argument with his employer, a successful farmer named Thomas Murrell, and Crews was terminated. Crews and his wife left the Murrell property, but Mr. Crews returned to the farm on April 12, 1896, under the cover of night, and hid in the haystacks. When Murrell entered the barn, Crews shot him twice with his Winchester. When Mrs. Murrell came to investigate the noise, she too was shot dead. Crews then stole a horse and rode to the nearby farm of Morgan Murrell, Thomas's son, and shot him through the head in an ambush. The killing spree continued into the next day, when he stumbled upon a stranger named Miller in Indian Territory while fleeing. Seeing that Miller possessed a shotgun and thinking him part of a search party, Crews fired on him twice, killing him. Crews was filled with bird shot during the shoot-out and was later captured by a posse from Thackersville that same day. Crews ended up in Denton due to a request for change of venue, where he was ultimately found guilty and sentenced to hang. His last words were "Howdy, Mr. Murrell," when speaking to the son and brother of the murdered men. Crews was hanged. He expired after eight minutes. Crews has the distinction of being the last man ever hanged in Denton. Though he was hanged, he was hanged outside Denton County Jail, not at Old Alton Bridge. I found no evidence of anyone ever being hanged or lynched at Old Alton Bridge, nor have any Denton historians, though some longtime residences like former Argyle, Texas, mayor Yvonne Jenkins doesn't rule it out. In a June 11, 2003, *Record-Chronicle* article, "Old Alton Bridge Retains Magnetic Appeal," Jenkins points out that the first Denton County Courthouse was in Alton, and that it's possible some criminals may have been hanged from or near the bridge.

I have found one other name attached to the Goatman of Goatman's Bridge, in what is definitely the most untoward of all the legends associated with the bridge. In this version, it's alleged that an abusive drunk named Jack "Goatman" Kendall, created the Goatman of Old Alton Bridge, as well as the other goat-men of Texas and its neighboring states, by having sexual relations with his goats. The only place I found this particular legend was on an antiquated-looking website called HauntedAmericaTours.com, which is maintained by a purported necromancer, and several paranormal researchers from nearby Marshall. The fact that a Denton man's supposed fondness for bestiality is present only on this site makes the whole legend reek of sophomoric civic rivalry, in my opinion. The same site also suggests that he killed his wife, Myrtle Mary—the Goatwoman—and for reasons unclear she haunts the Troll Bridge in Marshall, a bizarre sort of Brigadoon-like structure that only appears by chance. Despite the outlandishness of this—even when researching as fantastic a topic as the Goatman—I did investigate the validity of what I could. There was a Mr. Jack Kendell present in the 1920 US Census in the Rockwall area of Dallas. His wife was a woman named Lela Morris, from Denton. According to various *Record-Chronicle* community reports, they visited Lela's parents often. I didn't discover the man's occupation, but I'd wager even if he was a goat farmer, the legend coming out of Marshall is all stuff and nonsense.

Goatman's Bridge has been frequented by paranormal investigations, the most notable of which was conducted by the Association for the Study of Unexplained Phenomena (ASUP), and is documented in the December 2007 issue of *Fate Magazine*. ASUP's founder is retired journalist and college professor Rick Moran, who wrote the article. ASUP's most notable investigation is of the infamous 1970s Amityville Horror case in Amityville, New Jersey, and the group claims to be the "foremost debunkers" of the book of the same name. The group descended on Old Alton Bridge with cameras, digital thermometers, and similar equipment. ASUP members witnessed a nontransparent, glowing, orange cloud drift across a trail near the bridge, while later in the night a different investigator witnessed a misty apparition in the vague shape of a person, though both incidents occurred away from video cameras, all of which were mounted to tripods. The group also documented various sudden unexplainable temperature drops of thirty to forty degrees, and a cold pressure on one investigator's arm. On a subsequent visit, one ASUP investigator said she witnessed a man on horseback disappearing into a stand of brush. No hoof marks were found on the soft soil of the trail. No goatlike apparitions were seen on either of ASUP's published investigations, but the bridge remains a hot spot for several Denton-area paranormal groups, so who knows what the future investigations may reveal?

While the reason for the start of the Goatman's legend in Denton remains elusive, this specter lacks the notoriety necessary for Denton to be considered the birthplace of such tales, if indeed, they are only tales. Denton's proximity to Fort Worth makes it far more likely that their own version of the entity was influenced by stories of the Lake Worth Monster.

Up until my research brought me to Texas, all the mayhem and madness surrounding the various Goatman legends—while fascinating—had proven to be little other than foolish, occasionally gory fun masquerading as fright. But between the Phantom's killings in Texarkana and all the murders, executions, and suicides my Denton investigation led me to, I thought that I'd experienced the utmost depths of inhumanity. Having finished with Goatman's Bridge, I found myself longing for allegations of Wisconsin werewolves and Maryland mad scientists. Unfortunately, I had one yet darker path to navigate in the Lone Star State.

CHAPTER 8
LITTLE DARLING

The Harris County, Texas, city of La Porte is home to a Goatman legend similar to many others around America. The legend involves boys and girls, a lovers' lane, and an angry old hermit. But the legend isn't what makes La Porte noteworthy in this regard. It's the abhorrent crime that likely spawned the legend that does so.

These days, Powell Road is a busy little street that becomes much busier once it joins up with Sixteenth Street. But in 1950, it was a lonely back road that dead-ended at a Galveston Bay beach. Needless to say, few people had reason to travel it after dark, so it made for a tremendous place to bring one's high school sweetheart. According to legend, an angry old hermit lived down Lovers' Lane. He hated not only the sins he believed were being committed by these enamored youths, but the sinners themselves. The old man would regularly attempt to chase away the young couples.

One night, the body of a beautiful young girl was found on Lovers' Lane. She'd been brutally murdered. The girl was interred at La Porte Cemetery, and the old hermit immediately became the prime suspect; however, he died shortly after, leaving the murder unsolved. Not long after his death, people began reporting a terrifying man-goat with eyes like hot coals. The creature would leap out of the woods and charge the cars of parked couples. It was generally agreed on by La Porte kids that this terrible beast was in fact the demonic spirit of the dead old hermit, trying to claim another victim. After that, Powell Road was no longer known as Lovers' Lane. Instead it became known as Goatman's Road.

Unlike the goat-men from Fort Worth or Dallas, the La Porte Goatman is generally considered to be pure legend. There are no known, creditable sightings, only this wild story. However—like with most legends—there is a grain of truth secreted away beneath all the lurid fantasy.

The words "A Little Darling Found Murdered at the End of Lover's Lane, April 21, 1950" are engraved on a tiny tombstone in La Porte Cemetery, but the body didn't belong to some promiscuous teenager, but rather an infant, only minutes old.

The tragic killing of the child known only as Little Darling was first reported in the April 22, 1950, *Galveston Daily News* article "Stolen Towel Clew: Murder of Baby Investigated Here." Two children, Ned Gurnell, eleven, and Arthur Drummett, twelve, were fishing in the bay when they noticed a small bundle near the water. After about an hour, the two boys investigated and found the corpse of a newly born boy wrapped in a red-and-white cotton bedsheet—his throat had been slit.

Police quickly arrived and discovered that the baby—described as having a head of full, red hair—was also wrapped in a towel from a Galveston motel and a Houston newspaper dated from earlier in the week. The straight razor believed to have caused the deep gash in the throat of the infant was also inside the bundle. The infant was examined by a La Porte justice of the peace, who stated that the child still had its umbilical cord and that its lungs were filled with air, proving that he'd lived, albeit briefly.

Police questioned the owner of the motel, but came up empty handed. It was believed the towel had been stolen long ago, and would provide no leads. The April 25 *Daily News* article "La Porte People Prepare Funeral for Slain Baby" states that a reward was being offered by the people of La Porte for information on the murderer's identity, and that police were investigating various recently pregnant women, including a court stenographer who'd been reported as missing since she'd taken a leave of absence due to her pregnancy. None of the leads proved fruitful. Little Darling's murder remains unsolved.

Considering that the earliest Goatman legends originated in the mid-1960s, and that this atrocious crime took place on what would become known as Goatman's Road, it's likely that elements of this incident mutated after constant retellings, until the newborn boy became a teenage girl. All legends start somehow—if only this legend had started any other way.

If anyone has any information regarding the murder of Little Darling, please contact:

La Porte, Texas, Police Department
Address: 3001 North 23rd Street
La Porte, TX, 77571
Phone: (281) 471-3811
E-mail: police@laportetx.gov

CHAPTER 9

CALIFORNIA'S BEAST OF BILLIWHACK

After my dark, troubling research in La Porte had concluded, I needed something bright, colorful, and fantastic. The goat-man of Santa Paula, California, offered just that—at least in the beginning.

In early 1941—just months before Pearl Harbor and America's entry into World War II—*Captain America Comics* #1 appeared on American newsstands. The cover featured one of the most iconic and thrilling images in the history of the medium: a star-spangled, masked man fearlessly plunging into a hail of Nazi bullets to land a meaty red-white-and-blue right hook squarely on Adolph Hitler's fascist jaw.

The bombastic Captain America struck a nerve with an American public growing ever more eager to enter the war in Europe. More than a million copies of the first issue were sold, and subsequent issues maintained those sales throughout much of the 1940s. Comparatively,

Time Magazine's circulation was seven hundred thousand copies per issue.

The comic's story centered on a scrawny young protagonist named Steve Rogers who's rejected by the US Army. Irrepressible, he volunteers as a test subject for defected German scientist Professor Reinstein. The professor injects Rogers with a serum that transforms him into a specimen of physical fitness. Gestapo spies learn of America's breakthrough and kill Reinstein, leaving Rogers as Captain America, the country's lone supersolider in the battle against tyranny.

Cap has influenced imaginations ever since—motivating the weak to become strong, to help the oppressed. But even the most inspirational of heroes can spawn monsters. A twisted version of this story tries to explain why an abomination dubbed the Beast of Billiwhack stalks the Aliso Canyon in Santa Paula, California.

Legend says the Beast of Billiwhack is a nine-feet-tall humanoid with the head of a ram. The shaggy white beast lurks in the ruins of the Billiwhack Dairy, only venturing into the surrounding citrus orchards to feast on an occasional rabbit. Mostly the Beast lies in wait, tending its long, razor-sharp claws for those special occasions when some foolhardy youngster enters his lair in search of adventure.

The principle character in the Beast of Billiwhack legend is one August Rübel, a very real person. Rübel was the Swiss-born son of a New York family. Upon graduating from Harvard, Rübel left New York for sunny California, where he entered several ambitious business endeavors, one of which was the establishment of the state-of-the-art Billiwhack Dairy.

The cornerstone of his dairy business was a world-famous stud bull named Prince Aggie. The bull cost Rübel $110,000 in 1922—that's more than $1.5 million by 2014 standards. All was going splendidly for Rübel. His herd toured the southwest, winning awards and praise wherever they went. Then Prince Aggie died, one day after the insurance had lapsed. The June 26, 1926, edition of the *Oxnard*

Daily Courier reports that Prince Aggie passed away from a twisted intestine despite the best veterinary care possible. This loss, along with rumored losses on land speculation, forced Rübel to sell the dairy in September of that year. He and his family purchased Rancho Camulos and relocated to nearby Piru. Rübel's misfortune continued, when—as legend has it—he vanished mysteriously in World War II's European theater.

Rübel's wartime death, combined with that exotic-looking umlaut in his name, led a lot of people to speculate about his real role in the war. Somewhere through the years, a story began to circulate that Rübel actually worked for the Office of Strategic Services (OSS)—the predecessor of the modern-day CIA—and had been put in charge of a team of captured Nazi scientists. Rübel's job was to coerce the men into helping the United States engineer supersoldiers to ensure an Allied victory over Hitler and his Axis forces. The entire project was allegedly housed in the basement of Rübel's old dairy.

The scientists eventually conceded, but they conspired together to sabotage the project. Instead of crafting a platoon of Captain America–style soldiers, the end result was a pack of grotesque monsters that quickly ran amok. The government shut down the project and killed all of the atrocities except one—a ram-like creature that escaped into Aliso Canyon. The monster eluded capture until the government assumed the beast had died, then it quietly returned to its place of birth—the now abandoned Billiwhack Dairy.

Superficially, this is a most outrageous legend, but much of it is highly plausible. The idea of manmade supermen wasn't just some fantastic idea concocted by imaginative comic creators. The idea had been around for decades.

Eugenics is the philosophy of bettering the human race by promoting the reproduction of individuals with desirable genetic traits. Eugenics originated in the 1910s and had become a huge part of Nazi Germany's social structure by the 1930s. In order to keep the so-called German master race pure, the German people were encouraged to carefully evaluate potential spouses for undesirable genetics. Even further, people with congenital disorders, birth defects, or mixed ethnic backgrounds were sterilized.

These days this sort of racial fascism is associated almost entirely with Nazi Germany, but America played a big part in popularizing the philosophy. A *History News Network* piece, "The Horrifying American Roots of Nazi Eugenics," illustrates how eugenics was first championed by many scientists from Stanford, Princeton, Yale, and Rübel's own alma mater, Harvard. Also, much of the early research into the idea was financed by American institutions like the Rockefeller Foundation.

As an interesting aside, the basic principle of eugenics is the driving force behind how we breed our livestock. Rübel's world-famous Prince Aggie cost the equivalent of $1.5 million because of his ability to produce offspring with desirable genetic traits, unlike the bulls that are destined for the slaughterhouse.

The horror of the eugenics movement wasn't fully realized until the end of World War II, when the Holocaust was exposed. Nazi Germany murdered millions of people because they perceived them as inferior, even less than human. They literally treated human beings like cattle.

Considering all this, the idea of creating a superior soldier through scientific intervention would hardly have been considered outlandish. It becomes even more plausible when one reflects on all the new technology that came about in the quest to win World War II. The advent of the atomic bomb single-handedly ended the war in the Pacific Theater, for instance. Unfortunately for the Billiwhack Beast, the only part of the legend that's truly outlandish is the idea that 1940s science could have created a ram-man.

Then there's the dubious mystery surrounding Rübel's death during World War II. Legend claims that the OSS sent Rübel to Europe on a clandestine mission, when he vanished inexplicably. According to the article "Rancho Camulos" on the Santa Carlita Valley Historical

Society's website, SCVHistory.com, Rübel was actually killed by a German landmine in Tunisia in 1943. Rübel was driving an ambulance for the American Field Service (AFS), the same job he had had in France from 1917 to 1919 during World War I.

An October 31, 2008, *Ventura County Star* article titled "Over Decades, Ongoing Tales of the Billiwhack Monster of Santa Paula Cast Long Shadows of Doubt" featured remarks from Rübel's two surviving daughters, Nathalie Trefzger and Shirley Lorenz. The two women spoke of their father only as a kind man who made the most of his short life. He hardly seems like an ardent OSS taskmaster, but then again, the OSS were responsible for almost all acts of American subterfuge and sabotage in World War II. The true conspiracy enthusiast would say, "That's just what the government wants us to think." But enough about Rübel, let's talk about the Beast.

Most sources credit the first reported encounter with the thing to a nine-year-old boy who trespassed inside the dairy with a group of friends sometime in the 1950s. The boy returned to his home with large scratches on his back that he alleged were caused by a monster that'd jumped from the shadows and chased the kids. This bit of information is never cited, and is likely just oral tradition. If the attack is real, it's possible the boys stumbled on a sleeping mountain lion, a real-life danger for residents of Oxnard County.

While it might have been a misidentified animal that attacked the boy that day—if indeed the attack occurred at all—the Beast of Billiwhack was real as far as the young people of Santa Paula were concerned. The *Los Angeles Times* covered the phenomenon in a November 4, 1964, article titled "There's a Beast at Billiwhack—but Only the Kids Can See Him." It should be noted that this is the first national article about a goatlike monster in a major newspaper that I have found, though it described him as half-man, half-sheep. The article claims sheriff's deputies found one young man on the property carrying a sword with which to slay the beast. Another boy questioned by deputies claimed he'd encountered a "snarling, hairy man in a hole." This alleged encounter could describe a Bigfoot-like creature in close confines, but it could also describe a mentally ill vagrant. The most amazing part of the article describes something right out of a Mary Shelly novel. A leaser named Dorothy Renteria once held off a group of forty-three Beast-hunting youths with a shotgun until police arrived to disperse the mob. The article doesn't say whether or not they were carrying torches.

While the *L.A. Times* article makes no mention of the supersoldier legend, it is interesting that the apparent height of the Beast's notoriety took place late in 1964. Earlier that year, Captain America returned to comics in *Avengers* #4 after an almost twenty-year absence. The Captain quickly became the star of the comic, generating a renewed interest in his earlier World War II–era exploits. Throughout the years to come the Avengers would battle many of Cap's old Nazi enemies. Perhaps these stories influenced the imaginations of youths seeking adventure at the abandoned dairy?

Omitting all the legends, the Beast is severely lacking in creditable, reported encounters. Beyond the information from the *L.A. Times*, there isn't a whole lot more. There's an uncited claim in several Internet articles about the Beast chasing a group of hikers through Aliso Canyon, but I could not verify it.

Despite a lack of evidence to support its existence, people still visit the Billiwhack Dairy, and a small portion of those people claim to encounter the monster, which—thanks to California's growing Latino population—is slowly becoming known as "Chivo Man." "Chivo" is Spanish for "goat."

If there is some goatlike entity living in the Billiwhack Dairy, it couldn't possibly be the failed result of a World War II supersoldier program. The creature would already be more than seventy years old. I couldn't imagine an escaped lab experiment would have a very long lifespan. A slightly more believable but equally hard to prove explanation would be that the Beast is supernatural in nature. A certain segment of Santa Paula believes that the Rübel family was cursed—and not just because of August Rübel's financial misfortunes and untimely death, but also because of his son Peter. Peter Rübel died in 1959 from a self-inflicted gunshot wound after losing a game of Russian roulette.

If there really was some sort of curse on the Rübels—is the Beast of Billiwhack its physical manifestation? While no one has ever offered up a reason for a family curse, any goat-man more than matches the archetypical description of a demon in the Christian tradition.

In the *Ventura County Star* article, Rübel's older daughter, Shirley Lorenz, remarked that shortly after moving off the dairy property she'd heard that it was haunted by a ghost, but her sister, Nathalie, had never heard the rumor.

Considering that 1964 *L.A. Times* article, the Beast is without a doubt the oldest of the monsters discussed thus far, however, it only seems to have recently taken the identity of a goat-man. Be it demon or botched army experiment, be it sheep or goat, the Beast of Billiwhack, also known as Chivo Man, will likely thrive as long as kids need mysteries to explore. But with that said, I doubt that all this goat-man madness began in the Golden State.

CHAPTER 10
KEEP OFF LOUISVILLE'S TRESTLE OF DEATH

While most of the goat-man legends I've written about thus far describe the creature as murderous—or at least highly aggressive—not one person has ever been seriously injured in any of the recorded encounters detailed so far, not even during the gun-toting Lake Worth Monster hunts of 1969. I wish I could say this was universally true, but the Jeffersontown, Kentucky, version of the Goatman has taken lives, even if in an indirect way.

Also known as the Pope Lick Monster—named after Pope Lick Creek and the trestle that crosses it—this monster has various origins attributed to it. Many of these are nearly identical to goat-man legends found all over the country, involving crazed old hermits, bestiality, and satanic worship. The most unique and popular of the Pope Lick legends involves a circus owner by the name of Silas Garner—a circus owner I can find no historical trace of, even with the help of the knowledgeable staff at Circus World Museum in Baraboo, Wisconsin.

According to legend, in the late 1800s, a strange satyr-like creature was said to stalk the vast woodlands of Canada. When word of this oddity reached Garner, he offered a handsome reward for its safe capture. Eventually, the beast was apprehended. The monstrosity proved a hit and became the star attraction of Garner's famed freak show. The greedy promoter made more than enough money to cover the hefty bounty he'd paid for its capture.

All was going magnificently for Silas, until one tempestuous night as his train rocketed through the wilderness of western Kentucky. The stars were blotted out, the wind wailed like a demon, and lightning struck the tracks, derailing the train. Everyone and everything on board was killed, except for the Goatman. Some versions of the legend blame the dark creature itself for the accident, its very presence a curse. Other versions state a darker, more fell power lashed out at Garner for caging the Goatman. Still others say it was merely a freak accident—pun probably intended. Regardless of cause, a ghostly circus train is often seen or heard thundering down that same stretch of tracks, destined to never reach the next town. Meanwhile, the Goatman supposedly ambled his way to Pope Lick Trestle, just outside of Louisville, where he's allegedly lurked ever since. Thus was born the Pope Lick Monster.

The area around Pope Lick Creek was once a popular make-out spot for Jeffersontown and other Louisville-area teenagers, and these youngsters were said to be Goatman's favorite prey. The monster is usually described as a large humanoid creature with furry, goatlike legs, alabaster skin, wide-set eyes, a Romanesque nose, and horns that protrude from greasy fur. Much like the Maryland Goatman, this creature is also said to carry an ax, though the creature prefers to kill in a much more passive-aggressive way. The monster is said to use a variety of supernatural skills to lure people out onto the trestle, including mimicry, telepathy, and hypnosis.

The trestle stands nearly 100 feet high and has a span of 772 feet across a landscape that's mostly comprised of fields and sparsely scattered trees. The structure has no safety railings or escape routes beyond leaping off the tracks, a jump that almost guarantees death. Once a victim crosses onto the trestle, the Pope Lick Monster uses its abhorrent physical appearance to frighten its intended victims, causing them to leap or fall to their demise. Sometimes the monster waits for a train to approach, then from beneath the trestle, holds its charmed victim down until the train runs them over.

It seems, though, that the Pope Lick Monster has used his various mystical abilities about as often as he's used his ax. Crossing the trestle became a rite of passage for cocksure high school boys attempting to impress their peers by tempting fate and challenging the Pope Lick Monster, particularly around Halloween.

Nearly every goat-man legend contains a poorly disguised dare. Each legend basically says, "A certain place is dangerous. This is what is likely to happen if you go there. Here is where you need to go for it to happen." Additionally, many of the legends describe the specific, dangerous actions necessary to encounter a goat-man, as illustrated with the Pecan Creek Trail goat-man in Hamilton, Texas. This legend says you actually have to crawl inside a drainage pipe to encounter the creature, something I strongly advise against. As dangerous as that is, it doesn't even register when compared to venturing onto the Pope Lick Trestle. The hills and woods reduce the noise made by approaching locomotives, and the tracks around Louisville are still heavily trafficked.

In 1988, a black-and-white short film titled *The Legend of the Pope Lick Monster,* created by Louisville-area filmmaker Ron Schildknecht, was released. In the film, a character recalls his mischievous teenage years in 1980s Louisville, in which he and several others get their hands on a sixer of beer and head to the trestle to challenge the Sheepman—an alias sometimes given to the Pope Lick Monster, as it's occasionally described as having a sheeplike face and dirty, yellow-white wool. The film suggests the monster is the malformed progeny of a farmer who cared too deeply for his herd. I assume the director picked the lesser-used Sheepman moniker simply because sheep are more often used in crude barnyard humor. You know the sort—"Phil's from the state next door! Where the men are men and the sheep are scared to death!" While definitely juvenile, it is a sensible choice considering the film's protagonists are drunken high school students. As the film climaxes, one of the teens encounters Sheepman on the trestle and ends up holding onto the side of a railroad tie as a train screams by—an impossible feat given the amount of vibration caused during the five to ten minutes a train needs to clear a trestle this size.

In 1986—one week into filming—a high school boy fell to his death from the trestle. According to the March/April 1989 *Visual Art Review* article "Ron Schildknecht and the Pope Lick Monster," the incident gave a clear direction to the film. Instead of the film's characters simply wandering out to the trestle to look for the monster, the story was told in a flashback, ensuring the script had a cautionary quality.

As news of the film's production became public, the project was met with almost instant controversy. Various newspaper articles report Schildknecht was beset with phone calls from Louisville-area mothers and angry railroad officials who were worried the film would glamorize the legend and lead more kids to their doom. The article "Film Brings Deadly Legend Alive" from the March, 18, 1989, *College Heights Herald* states Schildknecht was threatened with lawsuits, and a warning from the Norfolk Southern Railway had to be read prior to screening. The article also states that the 1986 victim's mother was present at the premier, and according to Schildknecht, she said she got an understanding of what her son's final moments may have been like. That same night, two boys were arrested for trespassing at the trestle, and Norfolk Southern replaced the "trampled chicken-wire fence" with a ten-foot-high chain-link security fence.

The December 30, 1988, *Louisville Courier-Journal* ran a front-page article entitled "Trestle of Death," in which it records two more tragedies. Jack "JC" Charles Bahm II, a seventeen-year-old Spalding University student, was struck and killed by a train February 18, 1987, while crossing the trestle. He has since been eulogized at the site of his death. "JC, we love and miss you" is extolled in spray paint on the trestle's base. In May, 1987, nineteen-year-old David Wayne Bryant died of injuries obtained in 1986, when he jumped from the trestle to dodge an oncoming locomotive. The article doesn't specify if Bryant's injuries were obtained during the fatal 1986 incident, or if they occurred during a separate incident.

Individuals who grew up around Louisville, Jeffersontown, and the surrounding areas give the usual statement that the legend has existed for as long as they can remember. In the late 1980s, Schildknecht, who says he interviewed 150 people before making his film, proclaims in various interviews that the legend has been around for "three generations"—which, if true, would make Jeffersontown's monster older than the legend of Maryland's Goatman. The October 31, 1990, edition of *The New Voice* ran an article called "The Monster at Pope Lick," in which they interviewed Mary Ruckriegel, wife of then Jeffersontown mayor Daniel Ruckriegel. Mrs. Ruckreigel states she remembers first learning of the legend in the early 1960s. Just by using Internet search engines, I found various articles and blogs in which the author has a parent or grandparent who once foolishly crossed the Pope Lick Trestle. While I have found no official tally of the number of people who have died or been injured on the trestle, various sources claim there had been many more than three killed by the 1980s. One has to wonder why it took a short film to warrant the installation of an effective security fence. Trespassing at Pope Lick Trestle was a behavior that should have been discouraged at least two decades earlier.

Despite the security fence, people are still imprudent enough to journey onto the Pope Lick Trestle to tempt fate. In 2000, a nineteen-year-old Mount Washington man named Nicholas Jewell was shaken from the trestle by a train's vibrations. Much like the lead character in *The Legend of the Pope Lick Monster*, Jewell had attempted to hang from the side of the trestle to avoid a collision. His fall was fatal.

Unlike in Maryland or Texas, there have been no highly publicized monster panics with J-Town's local bogeyman. Because of this, the prevalent attitude in Jeffersontown is that the Pope Lick Monster is simply an urban legend that has woefully taken far too many lives. While all the origin stories of the Pope Lick Monster are unbelievable to say the least, that doesn't mean there may not be a grain of truth hidden within the bunkum.

In December, 2013, I interviewed David Lewis, a retired gentleman who grew up in Fern Creek, a once rural community roughly ten minutes to the south of the Pope Lick Trestle. Fern Creek officially became part of Louisville in 2003. Contrary to popular belief, David and his high school classmates had always heard that the monster resided at a small concrete bridge on South Pope Lick Road near the trestle, rather than the trestle itself. He and other Fern Creek youths would frequent this bridge late at night with the hopes of catching a glimpse of the monster. One night while visiting the bridge in either 1964 or 1965, David and his classmates saw what he believes was the Pope Lick Monster.

"To the left of the bridge, I could see him down in a [hollow] trying to hide behind a tree. He had white hair all over his body and red-looking eyes—it looked like a man. It never came toward us. Also it did not have horns, as some would have people to believe. It looked like a Bigfoot with white hair all over it. It was between six feet and six feet, five inches tall. It stood like a man."

While it's entirely possible a prankster would hide out at a well-known monster haunt to scare thrill-seeking teenagers, this wasn't David's only encounter with the creature. A few weeks after this, he saw it a few hundred yards away from the initial sighting, climbing the railing of a different small bridge.

While sightings of this Bigfoot-like animal never sparked a media frenzy, David recalls hearing stories of two other encounters during

Goatman: Flesh or Folklore?

his teenage years. According to rumor, the thing was once seen by a Jeffersontown policeman. When the officer reported the incident, his sanity was questioned, ultimately resulting in his termination. The second event involved a man who visited the bridge where David originally saw the creature. Story says he'd parked his motorcycle on the bridge in hopes of a sighting. When the Pope Lick Monster appeared, terror seized him. He frantically tried to start his bike, but in true horror-movie-cliché style, he couldn't get it to start. The monster got close enough to dig claw marks into the man's back before the bike eventually started and he sped away into town.

Curious to find out which legend was circulating in the mid-1960s, I asked David if he'd heard the popular legend that the Pope Lick Monster was an escaped circus freak. His reply mirrored the version of the legend Schildknecht chose for his film.

"I just in the past few years heard it referred to as the Goatman. It's always been called the Pope Lick Monster, and it's part sheep. Not goat.

"I only heard [the legend about the circus train] in the last few months. Rumor has it a farmer near the bridge had sex with a sheep and created the Pope Lick Monster. The farmer used to come out and shoot a shotgun at people on the bridge. But I never had that happen to me. My guess is the Pope Lick Monster is dead now from old age."

Beyond David's encounter, several paranormal websites reference an incident in which a Boy Scout group was chased from their campsite near Pope Lick Creek when the monster pelted their tents with stones. This alleged incident coincides with behavior exhibited by the Lake Worth Monster in Texas, as well as being a common phenomenon recorded throughout the years in relation to Bigfoot or other alleged Bigfoot-like creatures, but I was unable to substantiate the incident.

Is it possible that some unknown species of animal wandered into Jeffersontown during the 1960s and fed the legends? According to

Jeffery Scott Holland's book, *Weird Kentucky*, a creature similar to the one David described was seen in October, 1980, in Eastern Kentucky's Mason County. The Charles Fulton family was watching television in their home one evening when they were interrupted by a loud bang from their front porch, accompanied by the sound of a distraught chicken. When Charles looked out the door, he saw an apelike creature covered in long white hair carrying one of his roosters. Charles chased after the animal and fired at it with a .22 caliber pistol, but it escaped with its pilfered poultry. In November of that same year, a truck driver named Noble Clay saw a similar creature on the side of a highway and reported it to locals over his CB radio as a possible zoo escapee. Sightings of anomalous white-haired bipedal creatures are common in this part of the United States, as we'll see in the following chapters.

When I asked David Lewis if he recalled any association between the Pope Lick Monster and the trestle during his youth, he commented, "The story about the trestle was that you can hear a woman scream at midnight. Rumor says she tried to cross it and a train came along and killed her." In Maryland the legend of the Goatman became so popular that it eventually overshadowed a preexisting Crybaby Bridge legend in Prince George's County. Could these alleged creature sightings at a less-than-impressive creek crossing have stirred imaginations so much that the Pope Lick Monster became associated with the fearsome and already allegedly haunted Pope Lick Trestle instead of one of the small bridges nearby?

While that's a question that may never be answered, some in the Louisville area do believe the boys were in fact coaxed onto the trestle by the Pope Lick Monster. A Destination America television show called *Monsters and Mysteries of America* devoted half an episode to the Pope Lick Monster in April, 2013. The segment focused on the final hours of J. C. Bahm II, and included interviews with his sister, Leigh Bahm Rice, and his mother, Sue Larue. Both women leaned toward supernatural enticement as a possible cause for so many people venturing out onto the trestle. Leigh went so far as to admit she'd dared to walk the trestle herself to try and better understand what happened to JC.

The trestle does indeed have a siren's quality. I began to fixate on the ominous structure as I researched the Pope Lick Monster. I grew adamant that I visit the place. Much of what follows is taken from an article I wrote for CultOfWeird.com titled "Pope Lick Monster." The article was one of several legend-trip articles I wrote during a legend trip to Kentucky. Portions of the text have been edited slightly to avoid reiteration:

On July 27, 2013, I left Louisville in search of the Pope Lick Trestle. As I turned onto Taylorsville Road, I caught a glimpse of the primeval-looking thing. The trestle ran parallel to the road, nearly hidden by the trees. I felt as if I'd caught a glimpse of an immense, sleeping serpent. I turned onto Pope Lick Road, and the trestle immediately towered some hundred feet overhead. The narrow, curved road had a surprisingly high amount of traffic when I was there, and with the road having hardly any shoulder, my only recourse was to park at a nearby gas station. As soon as I pulled into the parking lot, I noticed a Louisville Sheriff's Department patrol car sitting unmanned. I refused to be daunted by this; I'd traveled all the way from Wisconsin for this. There would be no turning back. Besides, I had no intention of going anywhere near the tracks, nor did I plan to scale any fences.

Despite my lawful intentions, I felt like a criminal as I navigated an astonishingly high amount of traffic to take pictures from a nearby bicycle trail. Next I walked down the shoulder of the road to stand beneath the trestle. I felt a strong need to gaze up. As I did, the afternoon sunlight coursing through the ties was dazzling. I felt dizzy standing on the uneven shoulder of the road. My imagination conjured up the approach of a train, and I was reminded how certain members of the Jeffersontown and Louisville community believe a supernatural force did persuade those kids out onto the track. After a long while, I walked back to my car. My shoulders felt heavy. I took a final look at the antiquated, foreboding structure, and I couldn't put myself in those kids' shoes at all. Having been a nervous and meek teenager, I couldn't imagine needing a thrill so badly that I'd wander out onto that trestle.

Personally, I believe that the Pope Lick Monster *is* responsible for the deaths at Pope Lick Trestle. While there doesn't appear to be a body of satyr sightings, nor has any data been collected to prove a supernatural entity lurks around the trestle, the idea of such a fantastic being in and of itself is more than enough to tempt adventurous youths who are often cursed with a false sense of immortality.

If I may attempt to lighten the mood, I'd like to point out that the Pope Lick Monster is the only goat-man that has a legend that portrays the creature as a would-be savior. One variant says the Pope Lick Monster appears to people crossing the trestle in an attempt to warn them about oncoming trains. However, the creature's terrifying physical appearance either causes them to fall to their death or distracts them from the real danger. While always ineffectual in his attempt to save lives, at least his intentions are good.

A few paranormal websites theorize that the monster is no longer at the trestle. Louisville's urban sprawl has allegedly driven the thing south to the Jefferson Memorial Forest. Whether the Pope Lick Monster is fact or fiction, whether it's still haunting the trestle or shambling around in the woods somewhere, please, please, keep off the Pope Lick Trestle.

The Pope Lick Monster is an excellent candidate as the entity or legend that spread goat-man stories around America, but it's lacking one important thing—documentation. No one has yet reliably pinpointed exactly when the first stories of the creature began circulating.

CHAPTER 11
PENNSYLVANIA'S SHEEPMAN RUNS AMOK

Situated 450 miles to the northeast of Louisville, Kentucky, is Erie, Pennsylvania. These two cities are immensely different. Louisville is a sprawling metropolis that thrives off such white-collar industries as health insurance and medical science. Louisville is the home of such summertime institutions as the Louisville Slugger baseball bat, Kentucky Fried Chicken, and the Kentucky Derby. When someone thinks of Louisville, they think of green fields, warm sun, and business casual. Erie, on the other hand, is a rigidly gridded city in the midst of America's Snow and Rust Belts. Only in recent years has this industrial center pulled itself from the depression it suffered when America's steel and heavy manufacturing industries all but vanished.

Despite being as different as can be, they have at least one strange similarity—a creature called Sheepman that stalks their outlying suburbs. While Louisville's Pope Lick Monster is better known as a goat-man today, the relatively obscure Sheepman of Waterford still retains his ovine identity, despite the occasional accusation of being half-goat.

The Sheepman of Waterford is usually described as being a six-foot-tall bipedal creature covered in light-gray fur. The creature's most distinctive characteristics are a set of razor-sharp claws and ram-like horns growing out of a misshapen head. The creature allegedly lived in a cave on then-secluded Baghdad Road but occasionally ventured into town to terrorize teens on the east side of town at the Waterford Covered Bridge, also known as the Old Kissing Bridge.

Tales of the Waterford Sheepman seem to have materialized in the 1970s, the era in which most Goatman legends or sightings outbreaks reached their peak. However, Sheepman experienced a bit of a renaissance during the 2012 Halloween season, when dozens of websites, local newspapers, and late-night news broadcasts revisited the creature's shenanigans. Nearly all of them boasted that the creature was seen by "hundreds of witnesses," though finding reports of such sightings was difficult indeed. Many of the stories featured an anecdote from lifelong Waterford native Herb Kinney, whose friend was attacked by Sheepman. According to Kinney in an Examiner.com article, "The Legend of the Sheepman of Waterford, Pennsylvania," two young Waterford couples were enjoying a late-night summer drive in a friend's dark-blue Ford Mustang convertible when it began to rain. The youths pulled inside a covered bridge known as the Old Kissing Bridge to put the top up, when Kinney's friend and the other boy were accosted by Sheepman. The kids fought off the creature and sped out of the bridge. Supposedly the Sheepman mangled the roof of the car to such an extent it had to be replaced. Kinney claims the incident was never reported to the police because the teen's parents wanted to avoid embarrassment.

Kinney's story is a classic Goatman encounter, but it's hardly reliable. Stories like these are what folklorists refer to as "friend-of-a-friend lore." While Kinney's story is secondhand information rather than thirdhand, urban legends are almost always of this nature. The truth of the matter could be the teens got into some sort of accident and blamed the damaged car on a local legend. Or perhaps the incident never occurred at all, and could have just been some wild rumor set loose on the community by Kinney's bored friends.

The same article features a quote from a Sally B. that makes an even better argument that the Sheepman was simply an urban legend. She claims the creature was rumored to live on a dirt road at her father's old farm, and described him as part-man, part-sheep, with a hook hand that would chase parkers away from his territory. Like many goat-man legends, here we have a direct connection with the Hook Man Lovers' Lane legend—but just like elsewhere across the country, just when I'm ready to dismiss a certain goat-man as mere legend, along comes someone who claims to have seen the beast.

Yet another person interviewed for the article claims that she saw Goatman on two different occasions. A woman identified only as Marilyn claims to have grown up on Baghdad Road, where she saw the strange animal cross the road in front of her twice. The second incident happened when she was seventeen years old. She was pulling into her driveway one night when Sheepman ran in front of her car and vanished into the woods. She says this was the most frequently described sort of encounter with the creature.

Waterford paranormal investigator and history buff Heidi Kirclich LaDow has investigated the legend herself and was kind enough to share her findings. After announcing her interest in the legend via the Internet, she received the following anonymous e-mail:

> *I will let you know that the Sheepman story, as far as I know, started in the vocational agriculture students' heads and the fable grew until the general public adopted it as a local legend. I heard of Sheepman in 1970, and as a seventh grader it awed me and others. [The story was] that a man could have sex with a sheep [and produce a sheep-man]. What started as a dirty little story grew into a small town legend. I ain't telling no more!*

It's easy to believe that all this began as some juvenile rib jab, but that doesn't explain the strange animal that enjoyed darting across Baghdad Road in the middle of the night. Perhaps some hoaxer would lie in wait for passing motorists? It seems as if it's all a moot point. As the 1970s ended, so did encounters with Sheepman. An *Erie Reader* article titled "Eerie Erie" theorizes that since a sheep's natural lifespan is roughly only a decade, perhaps the creature died of old age. A plausible theory, if the animal in question was an actual sheep, but it most certainly was not.

Assuming that Sheepman existed outside of the imaginations of Waterford's teenage population and that it was a flesh-and-blood animal, perhaps it migrated somewhere less populated? I recently came across a bizarre string of incidents in the Big Valley Amish community of Lancaster County, some three hundred miles to the southeast of Waterford. This outbreak is chronicled in the January 1974 issue of *Pursuit*, a now defunct newsletter published by the New Jersey–based Society for the Investigation of the Unexplained. The article only states that these incidents occurred in 1973, but given the activities and weather conditions described, we can assume they transpired sometime in late summer.

Allen V. Noe reports that two brothers bringing in a load of hay came across a strange beast "the size of a good heifer, gray in color with a white mane." Noe continues, "It had tigerlike fangs and curved horns like a billy goat, ran upright on long legs, and had long grizzly claws." When the team of horses noticed the creature, they bolted, throwing the two men on the hard, dry ground. The animal left no tracks on the parched terrain.

The next evening, the animal was spotted again some five miles from the original sighting, this time by a farmer clearing weeds. The man was startled by a "ferocious roar." He turned in time to see the beast charging him. The farmer instinctively tried to defend himself with the scythe he'd been using, but the creature tore it from his hands. Lacking any further options, he turned and fled. The next day all that could be found of the scythe was its blade and the bolts that held it together. It was speculated that the animal ate the wooden portions of the implement because of a salt craving induced by the then-ongoing heat wave. It should be noted, though, that this farmer stated the animal had three horns and a tail. Perhaps since this witness was attacked, he didn't get as good a look at the beast as the two brothers the day before and exaggerated its appearance?

On the evening immediately following the second sighting, the monster was seen again, this time at a third farm located roughly midway between the first two sightings. A woman out feeding her chickens heard a ruckus. She turned around and saw the thing stealing geese, one in each hand. The woman bravely gave chase, but the animal threw one of the birds at her with such tremendous force that it knocked her to the ground, allowing the terrifying thief to escape with the other water fowl.

Nothing else was ever heard of the horned menace of Big Valley. Perhaps some Amish farmer found what very well might have been Sheepman ransacking his livestock and ran it through with a pitchfork before unceremoniously incinerating the abomination. Or perhaps it continued its southerly migration?

CHAPTER 12
SHEEPSQUATCH

Since the 1990s, something that very much matches the descriptions of the Sheepman of Waterford and the strange monster of Big Valley has allegedly called the mountainous terrain of West Virginia home. Could they all be the same creature?

Kurt McCoy's fascinating and chill-inducing book, *White Things: West Virginia's Weird White Monsters*, is how I first became aware of the latest creature to join the goat-man pantheon—West Virginia's farcically named Sheepsquatch.

McCoy's book credits a woman identified only as Tess as the first person to report the monster. According to Tess, her encounter occurred "a few years ago" on a road trip through Point Pleasant, in Mason County. The sighting was originally published at Johnathan Moore's WVGhosts.com in July of 2004, which likely places the sighting from sometime in the mid- or late-1990s. Tess and a carload of her girlfriends were returning home from a trip to Huntington en route to Charleston, West Virginia, one snowy afternoon. As the car rounded a curve in a wooded area near Arbuckle, the woman glanced to her left. Standing roughly one foot from her driver's side window was a huge, white-furred Bigfoot-like animal. The passengers began screaming, but Tess was so curious she put the car in reverse to get a second look at the creature. Before the animal turned and fled, she noted that it had a face like a sheep, complete with ram-like horns. It stood upright, and had doglike feet rather than hooves. Tess notes that she'd not been drinking, and until that moment had been a skeptic regarding all things Fortean. During the years after the encounter, she and her friends began affectionately calling the animal Sheepsquatch. While I applaud anyone willing to come forward with such a bizarre experience, I do wish that they'd concocted a more dignified name for such a fascinating new creature.

If the town of Point Pleasant sounds familiar to you, it should. The town was home to arguably the most infamous and bizarre rash of monster sightings in American history. From the winter of 1966 until the winter of 1967 the town was terrorized by a moth-winged humanoid with glowing red eyes called Mothman. The monster was rumored to live at an abandoned World War II munitions plant nicknamed the TNT. The affair climaxed in December of 1967 when Mothman was seen atop the Silver Bridge just before it collapsed, killing forty-six people. The Mothman saga was popularized by John Keel's 1975 Fortean classic, *The Mothman Prophecies*. In 2002, a movie by the same name was released starring Richard Gere. While Mothman sightings have only been reported sporadically since that fateful afternoon in 1967, a gaggle of strange entities are still rumored to prowl the TNT, including Sheepsquatch.

Sheepsquatch's TNT debut is recounted in White Things. The witness was a former navy man named Ed Rollins. Many sources claim that this sighting occurred in 1994, but the only date I can attach to it is October 14, 2004, the day the story was originally published at WVGhosts.com. Ed grew up near Point Pleasant and was captivated by the Mothman sightings. After leaving the military, he began conducting his own research. He would make frequent visits to the TNT area. Rollins was walking along a creek bank near Bethel Church Road when he saw the animal. The thing broke the tree line by the creek and began to drink. It was huge, walked on all fours, and was covered in dirty, brownish-yellow, matted fur. Its head was long and pointed like a dog's, and it had small front paws. The animal had large, single-point horns like a juvenile goat's. Most peculiar, the animal reeked of sulfur. Rollins didn't attribute this to some demonic quality—rather he believed the smell could have been caused by polluted water from the gunpowder once manufactured at the TNT. After several minutes, the animal finished drinking, crossed the stream, and moved out of sight. Rollins quickly fled back to his car.

McCoy's book chronicles various other weird-white-monster sightings in the nearby counties of Putnam, Kanawha, and Boone that other writers have since lumped into the sheepsquatch category despite a complete lack of horns or other sheeplike qualities. It appears that the term "sheepsquatch" is becoming a catch-all classification for any weird white monster. I feel bad for weird white monsters everywhere.

But while the animals that Tess and Rollins each described both had sheeplike characteristics, they also sounded like two entirely different species. In fact, most of the creatures in McCoy's book have few shared traits beyond their lack of color. *White Things* is a menagerie of strange white creatures of nearly every sort. Some are Bigfoot-like, while others sound like monstrous canines or polar bears. While the book is a compelling and entertaining collection of encounters, it's a cryptozoologist's nightmare. While the animals vary in description, they range in size from two feet high to being taller than the tallest man. Some are bipeds, others quadrupeds, and still others have six or more legs!

Beyond the staggering amount of unknown animals that it describes stalking the woods of West Virginia, many of the stories have an unsettling supernatural element that places them outside the realm of cryptozoology. These entities are often vicious toward humans and livestock alike, vanish seemingly at will, have an affinity for cemeteries, and some seem impervious to physical harm. Stranger still, some of these creatures have the ability to cause their prey to hallucinate. One witness who thought he was mortally wounded by one these creatures found that his wounds vanished along with the attacking creature. This sounds a bit like hypnosis to me, one of the Pope Lick Monster's many alleged talents over in Louisville, Kentucky. A supernatural explanation is appealing, however, McCoy himself openly acknowledges the folkloric quality of many of the stories, and eloquently demonstrates how even the most mundane of unexplained experiences can become exceedingly fantastic upon subsequent retellings with just a few minor, subconscious alterations.

Sheepsquatch first received national attention on March 24, 2013, when the Destination America TV show *Monsters and Mysteries of America* dedicated an entire segment to the creature in its debut episode. The incident focused on the disturbing experiences of two young hunters named Dakota Cheeks and Ricky Joyce during July, 2004. The incidents occurred in Breckinridge County, Kentucky, more than three hundred miles to the west of Point Pleasant, West Virginia. While hunting, the young men discovered one of their dogs lying dead with a broken neck. That night the two were rocked awake as something violently shook their camper. Determined to kill the violent thing, the two fled to Ricky's grandparents' cabin for additional ammunition. They soon discovered the animal in an open field just beyond a cemetery. Dakota described the animal as huge and white—nine feet tall when it stood fully erect. It had long arms with clawed hands, but it held them up and close to its body similarly to a kangaroo holding up its forepaws. The creature charged the two. They fired on it and fled back to the cabin. They returned to the field the next day but failed to find the carcass. It seems the Kentucky version of Sheepsquatch shares the West Virginia weird white monsters' invulnerability as well as their love of graveyards.

One intriguing coincidence I've noticed is that many of these weird white monsters such as Sheepsquatch are observed in locations on or near the Ohio River. Kentucky's Jefferson, Breckinridge, and

Mason Counties are all located on the banks of the Ohio, as is Point Pleasant in Mason County, West Virginia. In both 2009 and 2012, advocacy group Environment America conducted studies revealing the Ohio to have the most polluted discharge of any American river. The 2012 study warned that one of the many chemicals being dumped into the Ohio is a cancer-causing solvent used in dry cleaning called tetrachloroethylene. Could these animals be mutations caused by years of industrial pollution? I've hardly the credentials to make such a claim, nor would mutation explain the supernatural qualities many of the animals seemingly exhibit, however, I'm going to be drinking bottled water the next time I pass through the area just to be safe.

CHAPTER 13
A DEATH IN INDIANA

I've often marveled at bridges and their nearly universal link to Fortean phenomena. I'd wager every town in America has some sort of haunted bridge legend. And as we've seen, more often than not, goat-men enjoy prowling near these essential structures.

The ancient Celts believed that since bridges were neither land nor water, they were a peculiar sort of in-between where faeries and all sorts of otherworldly entities could enter into or exit out of our world. Similar beliefs exist in nearly every culture, to a certain extent. While a connection between bridges and Fortean phenomena has never been proven, such a connection would explain why goat-men are so often associated with bridges.

Even if bridges don't actually have a secondary function as ethereal gateways, the idea that they are supernaturally significant is such a well-known concept that all of us are aware of it, even if only on the subconscious level. Even individuals lacking an interest in unexplained phenomena have heard a Crybaby Bridge legend, or been read fairy tales of trolls lurking beneath bridges, waiting to devour unsuspecting travelers. Thus, anyone concocting a campfire tale about murderous goat-men might choose a nearby bridge for the sitting of his or her cautionary "true story" to lend it believability.

A particularly infamous, allegedly haunted bridge is located outside of Greencastle, in Putnam County, Indiana. The Big Four Arch Bridge—named after the four railroad companies that use the arch-shaped bridge—is an open-spandrel trestle that crosses over Walnut Creek. The Big Four Arch Bridge is unique in that the pier columns of the bridge are hollow, whereas in most cases these would be filled with concrete. This creates small open chambers a person can crawl inside. Perhaps it is these chambers that make the bridge such a magnet for stories of ghosts and monsters. The wide array of graffiti found inside these chambers proves that generations of local kids have been venturing inside, looking for a thrill—either paranormal or sexual. While most of the graffiti consists of teenaged couples professing their eternal devotion for one another, one can also find the name Goatman scrawled in spray paint here or there.

While the legend of Greencastle's Goatman is hardly known outside the local community, at least when compared to versions found in Kentucky or Maryland, it is perhaps one of the best researched—at least from a folklorist's standpoint—thanks to the Indiana State University students and faculty who have contributed to the Indiana State University Folklore Archives over the years. The archives are the largest of their kind in the entire Midwest, and numerous Greencastle Goatman legends collected by students can be easily accessed from their website.

Some versions of the Greencastle legend say Goatman is the deranged ghost of a murderer who wore a goatskin, while others claim the Goatman is a demon conjured up by animal or human sacrifice. Regardless of his supposed origin, they all claim he haunts the chambers inside the Big Four Arch Bridge. It's generally accepted by most Greencastle natives—even many who've claimed to have seen the entity with their own eyes—that Goatman was merely a person in a costume pranking thrill seekers and romantics alike. The Goatman's antics are usually attributed to an eccentric vagrant who once supposedly lived in one of the many chambers, or mischievous students from DePauw University.

Despite the popular theory that the Greencastle Goatman is all bunk, teens still travel to the bridge in search of Goatman and the legion of other supernatural entities said to lurk there. The archives describes a hook man as well as a veritable legion of ghosts that are said to haunt the bridge. These poor souls are rumored to be trapped in our world for a variety of reasons ranging from railroad accidents, suicides, even murder at the hands of the infamous Hell's Angels motorcycle club. It's said many of these spirits can be heard crying out when you venture inside the dark, forbidding chambers of the Big Four Arch as a train passes overhead.

Thought I can't say if the bridge is truly haunted, once in a great while legends have a way of becoming reality. In 2012 the Big Four Arch Bridge joined the ranks of the Pope Lick Trestle as a location where the local legend claimed a life.

According to a *Greencastle Banner-Graphic* article, early in the morning of June 1, 2012, a group of Terre Haute and Brazil, Indiana, boys were exploring the chambers of the Big Four Arch, when a sixteen-year-old, Kody Allen Snyder, fell off the south side of the bridge. When his companions found him, he was lying face down in Walnut Creek. After CPR failed to resuscitate him, the teens tried to drive him to a hospital but became lost on the unfamiliar country roads. The teens eventually found a house and woke the residents for help. Snyder was airlifted to a hospital, where he was pronounced dead later that morning.

The article doesn't specify the reason for the youths' exploration—maybe they weren't looking for ghosts or goat-men at all. Maybe they'd just heard of the unusual chambers inside the Big Four Arch and decided to investigate. No matter the reason, the outcome was tragic. Curiosity is a wonderful thing; without it we don't learn, and without knowledge what's the point of being alive? But curiosity must be coupled with caution. Hopefully future Greencastle explorers with learn from that tragic summer night; otherwise, for other Indiana youths, the Big Four Arch Bridge could very well become a sort of gateway to the world beyond.

Once again, I'd failed to locate the genesis of Goatman; all I found were a lot of wild tales and more than enough tragedy.

CHAPTER 14

THE SHAWNEE GOAT AND OTHER HOAXES

It was in late June, 2012, when my interest in Goatman first transcended Washington County, Wisconsin, and I began toying with the notion of writing a book about goat-man exploits from around the country. The idea came to me immediately before one of my annual two-day car trips to visit my family back in Georgia. My earliest attempts at gathering information were achieved by Googling Goaty on my antediluvian flip phone during the hours when my wife volunteered to drive.

As we made our way south through the rock-strewn highways of southeastern Kentucky, I chanced upon a website dedicated to a then-recent outbreak of Goatman sightings in the Kansas City, Kansas, suburb of Shawnee. The website was a minimal but slick-looking Blogger.com site titled *The Shawnee Goat Is Real*, run by a Shawnee resident named David Robert Harris.

The site linked to an archive of video and text stories about the monster flap from KCTV and the *Shawnee Dispatch*. According to these stories, the whole affair began on the night of April 3, 2012, when Shawnee residents Michelle Distler and Jeff Meyers were admitted to a local hospital after they began receiving visits from a large, black, talking goat, which only they could see or understand. The reporter emphasized that the two had been strangers to one another until that night, and that both had passed drug tests administered by hospital officials.

Another story, dated April 26, claimed that an ever-increasing amount of Shawnee residents were now reporting sightings of what a young, blond television reporter named Alice Barr proclaimed "the Shawnee Goat."

On May 9, two high school freshmen named Brendan Scullis and Andrew Westerfield entered the woods near their homes in Western Shawnee in the hopes of seeing the Shawnee Goat. As the two hiked along a familiar trail, they were physically attacked by a creature described as a "large, dark, half man, half animal." The thing knocked them to the ground and began clawing at them. Both boys were treated for cuts and scratches at a nearby hospital. Scullis received a deep gash on his bicep, while Westerfield was treated for a broken ankle and a severe asthma attack. The boys' parents were convinced they were assaulted by the Shawnee Goat, while Sarah Dooley, president of the local neighborhood watch, theorized some vicious prankster had decided to impersonate the so-called monster in order to commit acts of violence.

The sightings finally wound down later that month after a severe public backlash. The majority of Shawnee was of the opinion that those who had allegedly encountered the Shawnee Goat were either liars or mentally ill.

Webmaster Harris claimed sightings of the Goat had continued, but the media was ignoring the situation. A child's drawing of a black goat-man alongside his family was featured prominently in one of the blog posts. Harris expressed a militant, near fanatical belief in the monster and boasted that the site had been created as both a support network for those being visited by the creature and as a tool to collect and publish new encounters with the Goatman. Harris believed the creature could be a Púca—a type of shape-shifting spirit from Irish folklore that could take on the forms of black horses, goats, or rabbits, and were often omens of impending misfortune. A link to a YouTube video also implied a possible connection to the Greencastle, Indiana, goat-man legend.

Many hours later, we reached our hotel in the tiny town of Clermont, Georgia. I raced up to our room and sent off an e-mail to Harris, eager to learn of any new developments. Visits with old friends and the hubbub of family reunions soon took over, but each night I'd check my e-mail hoping for a response. Days turned into weeks, and still no reply. Soon, a combination of personal tribulations and various professional obligations forced my goat-man research onto the back burner. Months later, when I returned to the project, I again tried in vain to communicate with Harris. I passed the time by concentrating on older, more famous goat-man outbreaks, such as those from Maryland, Kentucky, and Texas.

Finally, as the book neared completion, I returned to the Shawnee Goat website for the first time since my 2012 road trip to make one final, desperate attempt to speak with Harris. I decided that before I composed an e-mail, I should reacquaint myself with the Shawnee outbreak for clarity's sake. I didn't want details from other goat-man events to contaminate my correspondence.

As I watched the alleged video broadcasts a second time, I noticed KCTV reporter Alice Barr occasionally glanced down during each report, as if reading from a script. I soon discovered that the woman in the video was, in fact, not Alice Barr at all. After a little sleuthing, I was able to trace the website back to a native Indianan and former DePauw University student who wishes to remain anonymous. Here is what she said, when asked about the website: "Never in my wildest dreams did I imagine anyone beyond my classmates looked at my silly fake blog. I created the blog for an experimental video class in 2012.

All of the videos on the blog are friends of mine from school, and every incident is totally made up. Shawnee, Kansas, is a real place, but that's about it [as far as reality is concerned]."

When I asked if the Greencastle, Indiana, Goatman had inspired her to select the Goatman as a topic for her project, I was surprised to learn she had never heard of the Goatman until she had already started creating her blog. Instead, she was inspired by a 1998 Internet parody site about a species of endangered cephalopod called the Pacific Northwest Tree Octopus, Irish Púca myths, and the 1950 Henry Koster film, *Harvey*, starring James Stewart. The film's titular character was a giant rabbit that only Stewart's character could see or hear. His friends and family thought him insane.

Unfortunately, during the course of our correspondence, Blogger.com deleted the Shawnee Goat website for reasons unknown to either the site's creator or myself. None of my e-mails to "David Robert Harris" ever bounced back to me, which implies the fake e-mail address the DePauw student used turned out to be active. Perhaps the e-mail's owner got tired of getting cryptic messages about bizarre goat monsters and asked Blogger.com to remove the site? Blogger.com isn't talking, so I suppose we'll never know the truth.

While the Shawnee Goat wasn't intended to be a hoax, this is a great example of how easily a well-crafted piece of fiction can spread legends like the Goatman in this digital age. Any person lacking in rudimentary critical thinking skills who stumbled onto this website could very easily believe it was legitimate. I thought Shawnee had a goat-man, at least for a short time. It wouldn't surprise me if years from now the teens of Shawnee began to whisper about alleged sightings of a bloodthirsty, talking goat-man lurking in the dark places near their homes, waiting to drive unsuspecting people insane.

While the Shawnee Goat is the most involved digital goat-man fabrication I've found, it certainly isn't the only one.

In the autumn of 2013, a friend called me up asking if I'd heard that there was going to be a television documentary about the

Goatman: Flesh or Folklore?

Washington County, Wisconsin, Goatman. I was certain there was no way a paranormal television documentary could be filmed mere miles from my home without me having heard about it. I thought perhaps she was thinking of one of the recent documentaries about the Maryland or Kentucky Goatman, but she was adamant this was about the "Goatman of Erin," Erin being a small community near Hogsback Road, one of the places the Wisconsin Goatman is rumored to live. Later that night I traced the rumor back to a baffling little classified-ads website called HartfordTradingPost.com.

The site is noticeably lacking in classifieds, but has a Hartford news section. The first story published is dated August 30, 2013, and is titled "Goat Man of Erin—TruTv Documentary." The article cites a recent incident involving a fictitious man named Duffy Cavanagh. Cavanagh gives a profanity-laden account of how he was sexually assaulted by the Goatman in the parking lot of a local pub following a night of drinking.

The article goes on to make the mind-boggling claim that the Vatican had given the documentarians permission to set up trap cameras and other paranormal investigation equipment outside of nearby Holy Hill Basilica. Apparently the blatantly satirical article has attracted a lot of Internet traffic. When I visited the article again in early 2014, the site claimed the entire documentary hullabaloo in Erin had inspired a commemorative Goatman of Erin T-shirt. The site warns that these T-shirts may only be available for a limited time. Now, I think, the site's true purpose is exposed.

A more recent "news" article on the site claims that a sword-fighting class will soon be offered at Harford Union High School. The instructor is a Mrs. L. Bobbit. The article was published in August, 2013, two months after the twentieth anniversary of Lorena Bobbitt amputating her allegedly abusive husband's penis with a kitchen knife.

UrbanCryptids.com is another satirical site that sometimes fools the foolish. The site seems to be based out of Springfield, Missouri, and mixes posts about famous Fortean events with blatant satire. The best example is a photograph of a hazardous-voltage sign that depicts a cartoon of an anthropomorphic electrical shock attacking a humanlike stick figure. The site alleges this could be evidence of a new type of cryptid.

On May 19, 2013, the site published an article entitled "The Mysterious Goat Man." The article features a sepia-tone antique photograph of three well-dressed men sitting in front of a log cabin, accompanied by a man wearing a goat mask, smoking a pipe. The article alleges this goat-man could be an ancestor of those encountered in Maryland and Kentucky, and that it has ties to a Freemasons-like organization called the Fraternal Order of the Seekers, a group that doesn't seem to exist outside of their website. The website sells "handy cryptid hunting equipment" such as T-shirts, bumper stickers, and coffee mugs. The website also links to a zombie apocalypse survival website.

While the Internet has always been a wonderful place to spread rumors, hearsay, and outright deceptions, the recent phenomenon of "creepypasta" is the Internet's latest and greatest attempt at polluting the world of Fortean investigation. The term creepypasta is a mutation of the term "copypasta," which itself is derived from the phrase "copy and paste," which is primarily how these stories pass from one person to the next. To simplify this for those who don't spend their every waking hour online, creepypastas are short fiction or flash fiction horror stories designed to spread virally via e-mail, message boards, and social networking sites. These stories always profess to be real-life experiences, and are primarily paranormal in nature. Usually the author either obscures or outright hides his or her identity for the sake of effect. Essentially, creepypastas are premeditated, digital urban legends. The Goatman was featured in one of these creepypastas. Titled "Anasi's Goatman Story," the "pasta" was originally posted on 4chan.org's paranormal message board, /x/, and was later republished in 2012 at Creepypasta.Wikia.com. In this grammatically incorrect, profanity-laced story, a mute, shape-shifting Goatman infiltrates and terrorizes a group of Alabama teens during a weekend at an isolated cabin.

Already, some of these pastas have seeped into real life. On several occasions I've been asked by enthusiastic but misinformed devotees of the unexplained if I've any information on an entity called Slender Man. Slender Man is a tall, thin humanoid with a featureless face who wears a black suit. Slender Man enjoys abducting and terrorizing people, especially small children. He's also nothing more than a creepypasta created by Eric Knudsen on the forums of SomethingAwful.com.

Slender Man has been dreadfully successful at convincing certain individuals that he's more than mere fiction. In June, 2014, two twelve-year-old Waukesha, Wisconsin, girls stabbed another young girl multiple times in an attempt to sacrifice the girl to earn Slender Man's favor. While I suspect something far more troubling was going on in these children's lives than reading some scary stories on the Internet, it's a stellar example of why we must always question any information we encounter.

This is especially true when dealing with Fortean topics such as Goatman. Was that snorting from the bushes that someone heard a monster or merely an alarmed deer? One needs to think even more critically while navigating the wilds of the Internet. Is the author merely too lazy to cite his or her story, or has it been invented out of whole cloth? Contrary to popular belief, not everything you read on the Internet is true.

The Internet is an amazing tool, but just like any tool, it's only effective if we use it properly. The Net gives us the ability to share information—and lies—in seconds. It's up to each of us to decide how it should be used.

CHAPTER 15
PURGATORY, MICHIGAN

According to Catholicism, purgatory is a sort of temporary hell—it's where quasigood people end up who aren't quite holy enough for heaven. After the appropriate amount of pain and suffering purifies these so-so souls, only then are they allowed entry into paradise. Conversely, residents of Michigan's Cass and St. Joseph's Counties believe Purgatory is a place some souls never leave.

Purgatory is southeastern Michigan's answer to the *Twilight Zone*. Officially known as Three Rivers Game Area, Purgatory has it all. There's a Dead Man's Curve, the ruined foundations of a mansion that was allegedly owned by Al Capone, and a large bleeding stone called Blood Rock, where Capone and his cronies supposedly committed a massacre; even a werewolf has been sighted there. And then there's Goatman. This savage satyr allegedly lives in an isolated shack located deep within the forest at a place known as Purgatory Limits. Story says those who seek the Goatman's shack will never find it, but the unwitting few who do chance upon it will never be seen again.

Information about the Purgatory Goatman—and Purgatory itself—was difficult to come by. The above information was culled from various Internet comment threads. Even the blogosphere, a segment of the Internet starving for new topics, has hardly any mention of it.

I contacted Holly Stephens of the St. Joseph's County Historical Society in the hopes that perhaps they had some information about the area. Much to my surprise, I was the first person to inquire about Purgatory. According to Holly, though, Purgatory has always been a breeding ground for local folklore. She described the location far more eloquently than I could. "It's a vast, tangled area—wild and basically used today for hunting…The roads [are difficult] to maneuver, and even my family, who have lived here all their lives, find it hard to get back to the same place twice!"

The general consensus among St. Joseph and Cass County Internet skeptics is that the legend came about because of an old hermit who used to live back in the woods. One Michigander I spoke with who wishes to remain nameless had this to say about the hermit hypothesis: "Just between you, me, and the floorboards, some pretty unconventional folk live near those woods. I wouldn't be surprised if one of them ended up being called a goat-man!" Another Michigander remarked that if anyone these days ventures out in search of the Goatman's house and never returns, it's far more likely they were victims of hunting accidents rather than a spooky satyr, as the area is heavily hunted and the season begins on October 1, right around the time thrill seekers are most eager to look for ghosts and monsters.

While I can't say that the people who live near Three Rivers Game Area are any more peculiar than people elsewhere in the United States, I too wouldn't be surprised if a hermit gave rise to the legend of the Purgatory Goatman.

A myriad of explanations has been offered to explain the Goatman's alleged presence at any given location, but nearly all of them offer a variation that claims an eccentric hermit is the root cause of the legend—some legends even claim certain goat-men are only crazed loners rather than goat-human hybrids. It goes without saying that a rustic loony is a far more plausible explanation than Satanism, bestiality, or science run amok creating a goat-monster. The only failing in this notion is that most goat-man legends seem to have started at roughly the same time, all over America—the late 1960s. I can't fathom that enough mentally ill goat farmers dotted mid-twentieth-century rural America to inspire so many legends scattered all around the country. I still believed that all these legends had a common source; I just didn't know what it was.

CHAPTER 16
THE MYSTERY SOLVED?

By the time I'd finished with Purgatory and returned to Wisconsin, I felt as if my research had gone as far as it could go. I'd examined every major goat-man legend in the country—and dozens of minor ones as well—but I was still no closer to figuring out why these legends existed, especially since the most famous legends mostly began around the same time, nor had I found satisfactory explanations for all these alleged monster sightings. I began to wonder if I'd been wasting my time. It was a notion I couldn't accept.

I'd visited the Washington County Historical Society numerous times during my research, but out of desperation I figured I'd make one more trip before I gave up on the entire project. This day, longtime research center volunteer and amateur historian Eugene Wendleborn happened to be prowling around the labyrinth of files located on the third floor of the Old Washington County Courthouse Museum. Wendleborn is the sort of fellow every community in America desperately needs. Despite being in his nineties at this point, he has a near photographic memory and a sincere love for all things Washington County. He can accurately tell you the exact date when a chimney caught fire on a now long-demolished farmhouse, and who was fire chief when it happened.

Immediately after I told Wendleborn about my goat-man research, he asked which goat-man I meant—the legendary monster or a man named Ches McCartney. When I asked who McCartney was, Wendleborn described him as a famous vagabond who wandered America from 1930 until 1968, pulled along on a rickety wagon by a huge team of goats. *Eureka!* I thought. *This could be my missing link!* According to Wendleborn, McCartney—also known as "the Goat Man"—visited Washington County once, and once only, during the summer of 1949, and Wendleborn, his parents, and dozens of other people watched as McCartney trekked through West Bend. Along the way, his route took him not only very near Kewaskum's "Goatman Road" but past the Jackson Marsh as well, another location the legendary satyr allegedly haunts. Wendleborn concluded that when McCartney left the county he stopped for the night in Fond du Lac County, just outside of the community of Eden, where he spent the night in a small church. Other volunteers who were present in the research center that day also recalled going out to watch McCartney's journey with their parents. Wendleborn and I went through drawers and drawers of material in the research center, but could find no documentation of McCartney's journey beyond a photocopy of a picture postcard of McCartney in a relatively recent issue of the *Kewaskum Statesman*.

Taking to the Internet, I was able to find a reproduction of a booklet titled *Who the Goat Man Is*. Published by McCartney himself, the booklet was sold or occasionally given away to curiosity seekers, and summarizes much of his life.

According to the booklet, McCartney was born in the Iowa town of Van Buren, on July 6, 1901—though his age sometimes varied by decades depending on which day he was interviewed. He owned and worked a farm until the banks failed during the Great Depression of the 1930s and he lost everything. He then started to work for the Works Progress Administration (WPA), a project started by the

Goatman: Flesh or Folklore?

President Franklin D. Roosevelt's administration to provide jobs for unemployed men while improving the country's infrastructure. It was on one of these jobs that a tree fell on him, crushing his left side and rendering him comatose. Here McCartney makes the incredible claim that he was pronounced dead and taken to the morgue, only avoiding certain doom by waking up "on the undertaker's table." This sounds a bit like hogwash, but it was a story that McCartney stuck to his entire long life. The accident left him "crippled and worn out." At this point the only thing McCartney had left was his wife—a Spanish knife thrower he'd met while visiting New York—his son, a wagon, and eighteen goats. Refusing to become a burden on the state, McCartney hitched the wagon to his goats, loaded up his family, and headed south to his home state of Georgia. Within the first couple of days, his wife abandoned the family during the night. McCartney would spend the next thirty-eight years roaming the countryside, often dressed in goatskin clothes. McCartney alleges to have traveled over a hundred thousand miles with his goats, visiting every state but Hawaii. The arrival of someone as thoroughly odd as McCartney in any given town was often an event, and selling picture postcards as well as booklets about his life was one of his chief sources of income as he roamed the country—an income that he used to open his Free Thinking Christian Mission in Jeffersonville, Georgia, as well as a church in Savannah. Claiming to be an ordained minister, McCartney preached sermons of racial tolerance and the love of Christ to all those who'd listen.

My next step was to visit the West Bend Community Memorial Library to try and find any information about McCartney's journey through Washington County. I scoured every issue of the *West Bend News* from the summer of 1949, but couldn't find a single mention of McCartney, much to my consternation. I was able to follow much of his progress, though, thanks to newspapers from larger cities nearby.

The July 22, 1949, issue of the *Racine Journal-Times* carried an Associated Press article from Mattoon, Illinois, that trumpeted the

Goat Man's impending arrival in the Cheese State. McCartney—accompanied by his thirteen-year-old son, Elmer Jean—was leaving Mattoon and heading northwest. The article also mentioned that one of their chief sources of sustenance was goat milk, which the goats could produce a gallon of each day. By this point in time McCartney had been roaming the country for eleven summers, and was already becoming a bucolic celebrity.

The August 29, 1949, edition of the *Waukesha Daily Freeman* contains an insulting story titled "Hundreds, Holding Noses, See Traveling Goat-Man," which places McCartney in Oconomowoc, Wisconsin, on August 28 by way of the community of Dousman. Journalist John Suttner interviewed McCartney and his son, who were on their way to visit Charles's uncle in Green Bay before returning to Savannah for the winter. The rest of the article is mostly tasteless jokes about the powerful odor of the goats, and the McCartneys themselves. Oconomowoc is located just southwest of Washington County, and McCartney would have likely traveled Hogsback Road or at least came near to it since authorities all over the country detested the traffic jams that McCartney and his goats often created.

McCartney hit trouble once he got into Outagamie County, just north of Washington County, on his way to visit a cousin named Hommer Bunnel in the town of Shiocton—just twenty-one miles to the east of Weyauwega's Marsh Road Goatman legend. The September 9, 1949, edition of the *La Crosse Tribune* picked up an Associated Press article titled "Goat Drawn Wagon Ordered Off Road." An Oshkosh municipal judge ordered "the Reverend Captain Charles McCartney" off the road at the request of a humane society officer, and he was charged with cruelty to animals after admitting that he and his goats had spent the last two weeks walking from Georgia, on a route that took him through Tennessee, Kentucky, Indiana, and Illinois. McCartney's heard was sent to the local fairgrounds by truck, and would be cared for by the local humane society. Costs would be paid by McCartney, who had one week to rent a truck and claim the animals.

McCartney's odyssey ended reasonably happily enough. He appeared again in the *Waukesha Daily Freeman* in an Associated Press story out of Dublin, Georgia, from February 18, 1950, still in possession of his goats. The story said that McCartney was headed to Florida for the winter in his goat-drawn wagon. There was no mention of whether or not he got to visit his uncle in Green Bay.

These insults from the media and harassment from local authorities were fairly common occurrences for McCartney. Alabama survivalist and herbalist Darryl Patton compiled a book about McCartney titled *America's Goat Man (Mr. Ches McCartney)*, which he published in 2003. The book contains some essays by Patton, but is mostly comprised of newspaper articles and personal reminiscences about McCartney from journalists who'd encountered him during his travels. The book is an amazing history about an extraordinary person. While McCartney usually inspired an odd sense of wonder in the communities that he visited during his wanderings, several articles in *America's Goat Man* illustrate how cruel people can be toward someone as stunningly *different* as McCartney. On several occasions he and his goats were beaten by cruel passersby. He was often arrested on trumped-up charges to remove him and his animals from county or state roads, and on certain occasions his goats were even killed in the night for no reason whatsoever. It's a shame, really, as beneath all the grime he seemed to be a loving soul. In his self-published booklet, McCartney tries to explain his devotion to his goats: "The goats have taught me a lot in the past thirty years. They don't, for example, care how I smell or how I look. They trust me and have faith in me, and this is more than I can say about a lot of people."

If you're wondering whatever happened to McCartney, even after he retired his goats in the sixties, wanderlust would still strike him from time to time. According to *America's Goat Man*, he made his last cross-country journey in 1985, when he took a plane from Georgia to Los Angeles, California, because at the age of eighty-three he decided he was going to ask actress Morgan Fairchild to be his fourth wife. At some point he was mugged and savagely beaten, and it was weeks before he was able to return home. In the interim, his children feared he'd died. He spent the remainder of his years rather happily at a Macon, Georgia, nursing home until he passed away in 1998 as he was nearing his hundredth birthday.

I believe it's safe to assume McCartney is the root cause of most—if not all—of the other Goatman legends. McCartney was already a peculiar sort of folk character long before the term Goatman was used to describe Maryland's Goatman in Prince George's County. *America's Goat Man* contains numerous articles that have him wandering through Indiana, Kentucky, Texas, and Washington, DC—which is right on the doorstep of Prince George's County, Maryland—numerous times. Even in states where I've failed to find mentions of McCartney's wanderings, if there is any truth to his claim of having visited all forty-eight continental states as well as Alaska, it'd be safe to assume his appearance in those places would have stirred similar reactions.

The occasional writer has described McCartney's appearance as a hillbilly St. Nicholas. As a child, I recall being terrified of a mall Santa Claus to the point where I reached hysterics and had to be removed from the store by my parents. Imagine being a child and encountering something so utterly irregular as McCartney and his goats, the huge dirty beard, the smell of the animals and the man as well. It wouldn't take much for him to be morphed into a monster after only a few imaginative schoolyard retellings, picking up bits and pieces of the local culture, such as tragedies like Texarkana's Moonlight Murders or the Lovers' Lane urban legends like Hook Man that they spawned.

It is my belief that McCartney inspired the stories of Washington County's satyr, and probably every other goat-man monster legend as well. The monster then plays whatever roll it needs to within the community. For instance in Hubertus, Wisconsin, he's used to convince people to drive safely on a treacherous road, while elsewhere he's used to dissuade teens from having premarital sex, or to warn children not to wander too near the railroad tracks.

I find it ironic that after all the trouble the Christian church went through to eradicate any belief in Pan, or satyrs, it was the exploits of a devout Christian like McCartney that would prompt a modern-day resurgence in satyr lore, though of a most bizarre sort. McCartney, through no conscious effort, achieved what Robert Ogilvie Crombie and the Findhorn Foundation had attempted in Scotland in the 1960s with their books and seminars.

I believe this says a lot about what exactly these mythical beings are, and how they relate to us. Underneath all the myth and fantasy, satyrs are simply us humans when we allow our urges to go unchecked. Sometimes that can be a good thing; other times it can be very bad. Satyrs also represent a link with nature we've spent hundreds of years trying to eradicate. But no matter how technologically advanced we become, there will always be something primal buried inside each of us, something that longs to find a connection between us and the natural world.

CHAPTER 17
BUT THE MONSTERS REMAIN

While I'm of the opinion McCartney inspired the urban legends of many—if not all—goat monsters across the United States, this theory still doesn't explain any of the eyewitness monster sightings that have been reported in many of these locations. Are they all lies, hoaxes, and hysteria? Are they all misidentifications of other anomalous creatures such as Bigfoot, or perhaps some combination of all of the above? There is no easy answer to this aspect of my investigation.

Many experiences take place where there is no history of Bigfoot or other cryptozoological activity. Take La Paz County's Goatman of Parker, Arizona, for instance. Like in other parts of the country, Parker's Goatman is a legendary fiend that's said to terrorize parked couples and campers alike. He's described by residents as a scraggly-haired man with a goat's lower half who smells of garlic and putrid water. Legend has it one of his favorite haunts is desolate Shea Road, and that he's particularly fond of grabbing unsuspecting victims and screaming in their faces.

Goatman: Flesh or Folklore?

The Parker Goatman was the subject of a short documentary by Hemet Productions called *Goatman: Search for the Legend*. The film debuted in Parker at a vacant retail store on October 27, 2010, but has since gained a larger audience via HemetProductions.com. The film consists of interviews with La Paz County residents who grew up with stories of this local bogeyman, and ultimately climaxes with the documentarians spending a distressing night in the desert searching for the monster. The filmmakers interviewed a man named Scott Garrett, who, shortly after moving to Parker, had gotten lost one night while searching for Nez Road. Eventually, he noticed a figure in a field near the roadside. Assuming the silhouette belonged to a farmer, Garrett pulled his truck to the side of the road. He called out to the figure, which was facing away from him. Thinking perhaps the farmer hadn't heard him, Garrett spoke louder. The mysterious stranger turned toward Garrett's truck in a slow, mechanical manner, his arms bent stiffly out at the elbows. Garrett could then see the man had ram-like horns and glowing red eyes. Before Garrett sped away, he noted the thing had two furry, goatlike legs. It wasn't until later when he mentioned the incident to Parker natives that he learned of the supposed existence of Goatman. On a subsequent interview with the Hemet crew, Garrett stated that he'd started having nightmares about the creature since his first interview. He was of the opinion the creature was otherworldly in nature, going so far as to remark that he felt the creature had looked into his soul. Garrett told the folks at Hemet he no longer wished to discuss the incident.

Encounters such as Garrett's, as well as Sandy Grace's encounter with the vanishing Goatman of Dallas, and Jason Miller's run-in with the cursing, reeking Goatman of Kewaskum, Wisconsin, also inhibit my acceptance of the Bigfoot explanation. It is tempting to dismiss such sightings by relegating them to overactive imaginations influenced by an area's attributed legend, but to claim that either of these incidents could have been caused by a Bigfoot-like creature is even more difficult to defend than the Fort Worth skeptics' explanation that the 1969 Lake Worth Monster outbreak was instigated by a partially domesticated bobcat.

Occasionally these creatures are seen in locations where no goat-man legend exists, and therefore couldn't influence the observations of witnesses. Renowned cryptozoologist Loren Coleman pointed me toward an obscure incident that happened in the early-morning hours of December 11, 1982, near Lincoln, Nebraska. The incident is mentioned briefly in the article "Bipedal Humanoids in Nebraska: A Chronology of Events" in the April 1987 edition of Raymond W. Boeche's *Journal of the Fortean Research Center*. At approximately one in the morning, an unidentified couple was driving home from a wedding in Utica, when they saw a six-foot-tall creature that seemed human above the waist, and "goatlike" below. They said it had self-illuminating yellow eyes and likened the creature's appearance to depictions of Pan. The *Journal* entry stresses that "neither individual drinks, and their [reputations are above reproach]."

The absence of a goat-man legend in Lincoln makes this sighting far more compelling than many of the rest, because the possibility of a lie or hoax is far less conceivable here than in other parts of the country. For example, while it's easy to imagine pranksters dressing in satyr costumes to become part of an established goat-man mythos, Pan seems a perplexing choice for a hoax where no mythos existed previously. One would expect hoaxers to pick more well-known Fortean phenomena rather than a relatively obscure entity such as Goatman. One would also be hard-pressed to think of a creature native to Nebraska that could be mistaken for an ancient Greek nature deity. The incident, if it actually occurred, is utterly bewildering.

An even better example comes to us from the November 23, 1903, edition of the *Topeka Daily Capital,* more than fifty years before the earliest Goatman urban legends were suspected to have started, and only two years after the birth of Charles McCartney. Workers from a zinc mine in the town of Iona, Kansas, had a disturbing encounter with what they simply called "The Thing" late one night. One man saw what he described as a creature with horns, long hair, huge eyes, and an inhuman look, though it stood like a man. The men turned and ran screaming out of the mine. Three others ran to the site of the ruckus and saw the creature as well. The men described it as "a spirit, or the devil."

The Iona incident—along with three other American satyr incidents—are chronicled in the September, 2006 issue of *Wonders*. In 1839, a lumber crew captured a family of strange animals in Minnesota. Bostonian entrepreneur Robert Lincoln described the lone adult as resembling a satyr. The ultimate fate of these animals is unknown. On November 26, 1888 the *New York Times* reported that a huge, black, horned animal was preying on domesticated sheep and pigs near the Great Bear Swamp in New Brunswick, New Jersey. Even more tantalizing, the skulls of horned human beings were allegedly uncovered in Sayre, Pennsylvania during the 1880's. Based on the size of the skulls, the creatures were estimated to be seven feet tall, but just like the Minnesota mystery animals, the fate of these skulls is unknown.

I acknowledge that goat-man encounters are utterly fantastic, and often describe phenomena that challenge even the most open-minded individual to consider them objectively, however, these incidents must be approached, regardless of their outlandishness, as genuine experiences until proven otherwise. After all, the entire Fortean school of thought was created so that such phenomena wouldn't be dismissed because of personal bias or, worse yet, the belief that something can't be a real phenomenon because the current limits of scientific knowledge can't explain it. Moreover, consider that witnesses who report more commonly experienced phenomena such UFO or lake-monster sightings are often ridiculed to the point of self-seclusion. Imagine the taunts a goat-man eyewitness would receive at the office. The bravery these witnesses display in coming forward with what they perceive to be sincere experiences should at least earn them our sincere attention.

If even one of the goat-man sightings in this book is genuine, that means these creatures are real. In that case, one question remains to be asked: What are they? It's safe to say that if people are truly seeing half-man, half-goat creatures, they almost have to be supernatural in nature. There is no primate anywhere in the fossil record with either horns or hooves. It is also outlandish to put an alien spin on goat-men. The odds of any extraterrestrial life forms evolving in a humanoid, remotely familiar form and visiting earth sporadically with seemingly no other agenda than frightening teen-aged lovers, lost travelers, and turn-of-the-last-century zinc miners is beyond asinine. Of course, saying these creatures are some ancient nature spirits that occasionally materialize before unsuspecting humans is also outlandish, but out of the possibilities I've proposed, it's the least mind-boggling choice.

The biggest obstacle in accepting this notion, beyond it being so very strange, is that satyrs are a very Old World phenomenon. During my research, many have asked me why a Greek nature spirit would be roaming around any portion of North America. My answer to that is, perhaps at some point in history, creatures similar to satyrs were thought to roam North America.

In addition to the Piscataway of Maryland's possibly horned-deity Okee, around 500 B.C., effigy mounds of various shapes and sizes began to dot the landscape of Wisconsin and other adjacent Midwestern states.

The people who built these mounds remain mysterious. Known only as the Mound Builders, it's now largely accepted that they were ancestors of present day tribes such as the Potawatomi or Winnebago, but long ago this wasn't the case. Since the native population had forgotten both the purpose of the mounds as well as the identity of their architects by the time European settlers arrived, early European Americans began to theorize that a "lost race" was responsible. Dubious theories regarding these people's identities ranged from the lost tribe of Israel to refugees from Atlantis. While it is exceedingly unlikely that Atlanteans built these mounds, they are wondrous.

Many mounds are simple linear and conical shapes, while others resemble birds, turtles, and large cats. Some of the mounds were used for burial, while others severed a purpose that is yet unclear. The most intriguing of all these earthworks are known as "the man mounds," the majority of which were located in southwestern Wisconsin, in what is modern-day Richland, Dane, and Sauk Counties. Five out of seven of these huge mounds resembled men with huge horns protruding from their head. Nearly all of these amazing manlike earthworks have been destroyed, with the most notable exception being a particularly huge formation in Man Mound County Park in Sauk County. Before its lower legs were destroyed by road construction at the dawn of the twentieth century, it was 218 feet in length.

It's generally accepted that these works could represent effigies of shamans, who in more modern times often wore bison headdresses, or a Winnebago hero-god named Red Horn who was sent to earth to battle giants and evil spirits. All are highly plausible theories, but since we neither know if the Mound Builders wore bison headdresses or if they knew the tale of Red Horn, the man mounds remain a fascinating mystery.

Both theories are much more believable than my absurd little notion that these earthworks could represent a satyr tradition long ago lost to time, but after two years of researching nothing but goatmen, on my recent visit the horned figure at Man Mound certainly reminded me much more of Goatman than a shaman in a headdress.

If I may quote once again from Violet Tweedale's *Ghosts I Have Seen* in regard to Lady Wemyss's childhood satyr sighting in Scotland, "[Lady Wemyss] believed that much of the tradition of mythical creatures represented solid fact, and that it was possible there were failures of creation still extant. Again, might there not be races fallen out of evolution, but retaining as a survival certain powers that to us appear miraculous."

Perhaps somewhere out there in the invisible world, satyrs do exist, occasionally leaping through the vale to cause a bit of mischief before retreating back to wherever they came from, satisfied in the knowledge that we haven't completely forgotten them. It's my opinion that this possibility is no more far-fetched than a belief in ghosts, or aliens, or even a species of giant primates living in the sparse, new growth forests of the United States.

It should now be obvious that a surprisingly large body of goat-men sightings exists in the United States, yet they remain obscure. That's because no community within the world of the unexplained will take ownership of these goat-men, leaving them in a sort of limbo.

Ufologists—those who research UFO sightings—pay no attention to Goatman because no strange lights or aircrafts have ever been associated with the creature. Most ghost hunters consider him too much of a physical phenomenon, and therefore out of their field of study, despite many of the stories having an overt supernatural quality. Many cryptozoologists dismiss the stories as nothing more than modern-day folklore because of these supernatural qualities. They consider them mere fiction devised as a cautionary tale or a cheap scare. Folklorists collect the information, archive it away, and occasionally write an essay on the subject, but rarely, if ever, consider it could be a real creature. And who can blame them? Isn't that the domain of cryptozoologists? While this book has failed to ultimately answer its own titular question, if nothing else, I hope it at least encourages any of the above communities to actively monitor the phenomenon.

If after reading this book you're still rolling your eyes at the thought of satyrs gallivanting though suburban America, I can't blame you. Even after two years of reading and thinking about little else besides goat-men, I myself can't even entertain the notion that they might be real—it's just too inconceivable. I'd have to see one to believe it, and frankly I hope I never do. Seeing an entity like the one Jason Miller saw in the woods surrounding Kewaskum's Goatman's Road is so utterly fantastic, I fear it could unhinge my grasp on reality itself.

TIMELINE OF REPORTED CREATURE SIGHTINGS IN THE UNITED STATES ORGANIZED BY STATE

This timeline includes only eyewitness encounters with the strange creatures discussed in this book. Second- or thirdhand stories, otherwise known as "friend-of-a-friend lore," have been omitted.

Most encounters describe creatures that lack goatlike characteristics, but have been included since certain researchers believe Goatman is often a different cryptid that has been misidentified because of local folklore.

Excluded are any encounters with strange creatures outside of areas traditionally associated with Goatman legends. For example, in Wisconsin, only Bigfoot-like creature sightings that occurred in

Washington County are included in this section, though sightings of the creature occurred in multiple counties during the same brief period of time in 2006. Exceptions to this rule are if a sighting involves a creature that matches Goatman's description, such as West Virginia's and Kentucky's Sheepsquatch sightings.

Please note that some sightings that failed to appear elsewhere in the book for various reasons have been included here for completeness, particularly sightings in the Maryland which are abundant or similar.

Arizona
Date Unknown: While lost one night in search of Nez Road, new Parker- resident Scott Garrett drives up alongside a man in a field to ask for directions. When the man turns to face him, Garrett sees the man has horns, glowing red eyes, and hairy, hooved legs.
Source: *Goatman: Search for the Legend*, 2010.

Kansas
November, 1903: Zinc miners in Iona encounter a large, inhuman creature with horns, long hair, and bulging eyes. They describe it as looking like the devil himself.
Source: *Topeka Daily Capital*, 1903

Kentucky
About 1964 or 1965: David Lewis and classmates twice witness a large, white-haired, red-eyed, Bigfoot-like monster at two different bridges near the Pope Lick Trestle, in Jeffersontown, Kentucky.
Source: Author's files.

July, 2004: Dakota Cheeks and Ricky Joyce's camper is attacked in the middle of the night on a hunting trip in Breckenridge County. The two eventually discover an enormous, white-haired, Bigfoot-like creature with horns and peculiar, kangaroo-like forepaws. The two men

fired on it, but since it seemed unharmed by their assault, they fled to a relative's house.
Source: *Monsters and Mysteries of America*, 2013.

Maryland
1600s: Captain John Smith writes that the Indians of southern Maryland worship a fearful spirit called Okee (sometimes spelled "Ochre" in other sources). Smith refers to this spirit as the devil. He could take the form of many animals. It is said the Piscataway Indians of southern Maryland wore tattoos of "the monstrous-looking devil" on their breasts. Another passage claims that "the devil" appears to the Piscataway. Are these the earliest references to the Maryland Goatman?
Source: *The Maryland Bigfoot Digest*, 2004.

1600s: A drawing of a hairy "Bigfoot-like creature" appears on a map depicting seventeenth-century fauna in Maryland. Hairy bipeds like this are often seen in locations associated with the Goatman, or are confused with or declared to be the Goatman.
Source: *The Real Story Behind the Exorcist*, 2006

August 1, 1957: Twenty-four-year-old Riverty Garner and his young wife were pulling into their Upper Marlboro. home when they struck an animal that crossed in front of them. When they turned their vehicle around and pointed it at the animal, it reportedly looked like a gorilla, and its eyes were glowing red as it approached them.
Source: *The Real Story Behind the Exorcist*, 2006.

August 2, 1957: Garner's neighbor, Mrs. Francis Brady, sees a strange creature peering through a bedroom window. Mr. H. L. Brady fired his shotgun at the animal, and the Brady family temporarily abandoned their home and moved in with relatives. A six-day search for what papers dubbed "The Abominable Phantom" began.
Source: *The Real Story Behind the Exorcist*, 2006.

August 6, 1957: Two residents of Sansbury Road see the creature in Forestville, Maryland. The creature is also sighted in Forestville by a Walker Mill Road resident in Richie, Maryland.
Source: *The Maryland Bigfoot Digest*, 2004.

August 8, 1957: Mr. Garner tells reporters that he now believes the animal he hit was a neighbor's recently injured deaf and elderly Chow dog named China. The search ends with no evidence of the creature recovered by any of several search teams.
Source: *The Real Story Behind the Exorcist*, 2006.

1965: Mr. Jack Wimon is chased by a large two-legged creature on Tucker Road, future home to the Goatman legend.
Source: *The Maryland Bigfoot Digest*, 2004.

1967: Dennis Dunleavy and friends encounter the Goatman on Ardwick-Ardmore Road, in Lanham. This is the earliest recorded encounter with a creature in Maryland called Goatman.
Source: *The Maryland Bigfoot Digest*, 2004.

About 1967: Mitchellville's Cleary Family sees a "ragged, unkempt something" near their home. Mrs. Cleary calls in her children from playing in the yard.
Source: "The Legend of Goatman: P.G. County's Ax-Wielding, Dog-Beheading and Much Loved Urban Legend Makes a 90's Comeback." *The Washington City Paper*, September 18, 1998.

1968: A woman was forced to stop her car to avoid hitting a large hair-covered creature standing in the middle of the road in the Patuxent Wildlife Research Center in Laurel. The creature beat on the hood of her car before disappearing into the woods.
Source: *Monsters of Maryland*, 2012.

December, 1968: A woman witnesses a "Bigfoot-type" creature wandering across Route 197 at a farm near Bowie.
Source: *The Maryland Bigfoot Digest*, 2004.

January, 1969: A large "Bigfoot-type" animal walks onto Route 197 in Beltsville. Witness Audrey Havice is forced to stop her vehicle to avoid a collision. Route 197 comes within just a few miles of the Beltsville Agricultural Research Center, one of the legendary birthplaces of the Goatman.
Source: *The Maryland Bigfoot Digest*, 2004.

1970: An alleged "Bigfoot-type creature" sighting occurred near Lottsford Road in Mitchellville. Lottsford Road's "Crybaby Bridge" would eventually become attached to the Goatman Legend.
Source: The University of Maryland Folklore Archives.

1970: A couple parked on Fletchertown Road in Bowie see a creature they describe as half-man, half-goat.
Source: The University of Maryland Folklore Archives.

1970: Stanford Lizama and his girlfriend claim the Goatman ran in front of their car on Tucker Road in Oxon Hill.
Source: The University of Maryland Folklore Archives.

1970: Patricia Isidro and a group of friends drive down Tucker Road in Oxon Hill and see a pair of glowing red eyes which they attribute to the Goatman.
Source: The University of Maryland Folklore Archives.

1970: Two girls allege that the Goatman ran in front of their car as they drove down Tucker Road in Oxon Hill, causing them to swerve and crash.
Source: The University of Maryland Folklore Archives.

1970: The Goatman allegedly attacks a couple in a parked car near the bridge on Tucker Road, in Oxon Hill.
Source: *The Maryland Bigfoot Digest,* 2004.

October, 1971: Ray Hayden and Willie Gheen see the Goatman in a wooded area along Zug Road. It's described as being half-man, half-animal.
Source: *The Maryland Bigfoot Digest,* 2004.

November 3, 1971: A large shadowy creature was spotted outside the Edwards family residence at 8510 Zug Road in Bowie. The family had been awoken in the night by the barking of the April Edwards's new puppy, Ginger. The strange creature was seen roaming in a nearby field. The pup was found a short time later by the Edwardses' relatives, Ray Hayden and Willie Gheen. The animal had been mutilated and decapitated. The Goatman was blamed. Note that this event takes place just days after the Maryland Goatman is mentioned in a newspaper—an October 27, 1971, article about local ghost stories.
Source: *The Prince George's County News,* November 10, 1971.

November 17, 1971: Sixteen-year-old Kathy Edwards and several other girls reportedly saw the Goatman exit a pickup truck it had been seated in near Hayden's home and enter the woods. Police Captain Lawrence Wheeler noted that numerous Goatman sightings had been reported.
Source: *Prince George's County News,* November 10, 1971.

November, 1971: April Edwards sees the hairy man-creature once more, this time around the Hayden's Junkyard, in Bowie. She believes it was searching for food.
Source: *The Real Story Behind the Exorcist,* 2006.

November 24, 1971: Two carloads of teens block off Tucker Road, alleging they have the Goatman trapped.
Source: *The Real Story Behind the Exorcist*, 2006.

September, 1976: Ronny Williams was poaching deer in the Patuxent Wildlife Research Center in Laurel. As he climbed down from a tree stand, Mr. Williams observed a large, upright, hairy animal walking into a clearing and disappearing into the woods.
Source: *The Maryland Bigfoot Digest*, 2004.

October, 1976: Francine Abell witnesses a six-foot-tall gorilla-like creature walking in front of her car at a Highway 198 exit ramp to I-95 South in Laurel, Maryland. The creature had rounded shoulders, glowing red eyes, and gray-brown fur. When her car got nearer, the animal stepped over a railing and fled into the woods.
Source: *The Real Story Behind the Exorcist*, 2007.

March, 1977: A man identified only as a NASA engineer on his way to Goddard Space Flight Center reported seeing a large, hairy animal being chased through the fog by a dog. The animal supposedly stopped, grabbed the dog, and tossed it on Highway 95 before disappearing into the woods.
Source: *The Real Story Behind the Exorcist*, 2006.

August, 1978: A group of Pallotti High School students sees a "Bigfoot-like creature" near Rocky Gorge Reservoir.
Source: *The Maryland Bigfoot Digest*, 2004.

August, 1985: Mickey Bell sees a "Bigfoot-like creature" while rabbit hunting in Laurel.
Source: The Maryland Bigfoot Digest, 2004

August, 1988: A "Bigfoot-like creature" is seen crossing Route 381 in Aquasco.
Source: *The Maryland Bigfoot Digest*, 2004.

Nebraska
December 11, 1982: Late one night after attending a wedding, a couple encounters a peculiar six-foot-tall creature just outside of Lincoln. The creature appeared to be human above the waist, and goatlike below. The couple noted the creature had self-illuminating yellow eyes.
Source: *Journal of the Fortean Research Center*, April, 1987.

Pennsylvania
Summer, 1973: A rash of strange monster sightings occurred in the Amish community of Big Valley over a three-day span. A large, white-haired, bipedal creature with fangs, curved horns, and sharp claws attacks farmers and livestock alike.
Source: *Journal of the Fortean Research Center*, April, 1987.

Texas
July 10, 1969: First recorded sighting of the Lake Worth Monster (sometimes referred to as the Goatman), occurs in Fort Worth Texas. *The Star-Telegram* reports an incident in which a half man, half goat with scales like a fish leaped onto the hood of a couple's car one night while parked at Lake Worth. This is the first known newspaper article in the country to describe an anomalous-creature that was half-man, half-goat.
Source: *Fort Worth Star-Telegram*, July 10, 1969.

July 11, 1969: The Lake Worth Monster was sighted again after midnight on July 11 by Jack Harris, who witnessed the creature crossing a road that led into the Lake Worth Nature Center. About twenty to thirty people watched as it hurled a tire some five hundred feet toward the crowd from a bluff. The animal was described by Harris

as seven feet tall, three hundred pounds, and covered in whitish-gray fur.
Source: *Fort Worth Star-Telegram*, July 11, 1969.

July 14, 1969: A man named Mike Kinson reports that in addition to having witnessed misty apparitions at Lake Worth, he's also seen the Lake Worth Monster.
Source: *Fort Worth Star-Telegram*, July 14, 2006.

Summer, 1969: Allan Plaster and a friend encounter the Lake Worth Monster one night while driving near the lake in search of the creature. Plaster snaps a grainy black-and-white Polaroid photograph of the large, hairy, white, Bigfoot-like creature.
Source: *Fort Worth Star-Telegram*, June 8, 2006.

November 7, 1969: Charles Buchanan was asleep in a sleeping bag in the back of his pickup truck at Lake Worth when he was awakened in the middle of the night by a large creature lifting him into the air. Buchanan was able to give the thing a bag of leftover chicken that was lying nearby. The monster then swam away toward Greer Island.
Source: *Mysterious* America, 1983.

December 17, 1976: Three men visited Greer Island at Lake Worth, Texas, to drink beer. While facing north, the three heard extremely loud vocalizations that lasted three seconds each with a three-second pause between each. One man described the sound as so loud it echoed, and said that it felt as if the woods were shaking.
Source: *BFRO Report #35721*. BFRO.net, 2014.

1990s: While hiking to meet his friends, Mount Nebo teenager Doug Sheldon encounters a goatlike bipedal monster howling in a moonlit field. Later that night Sheldon finds his friends in town, but they

don't believe his story. The group travels back to the field and again sees the creature.
Source: *Monsters and Mysteries of America*, 2013.

Mid-August, 2001: Sandy Grace was jogging on a trail that meandered around Dallas's White Rock Lake around two o'clock in the afternoon. She noticed a large horned creature covered in coarse brown hair in the woods. The creature approached her with a menacing grin. It got within a dozen or so feet of her, then there was a blinding flash of light and the entity vanished. Grace noted that before she saw the creature she was overcome by what she could only describe as a panic attack.
Source: *Monsters of Texas*, 2010.

Summer, 2005: Writers Nick Redfern and Ken Gerhard find strange structures in the woods around Lake Worth, which they refer to as "Bigfoot teepees." These strange creations are usually found in areas where Bigfoot-like creatures have been seen.
Source: *Monsters of Texas*, 2010.

West Virginia
Mid- or late-1990s: A woman named Tess and several friends are driving through Point Pleasant one snowy afternoon when they see an enormous Bigfoot-like creature with ram-like horns and a sheep's face standing alongside the road.
Source: *White Things*, 2008.

October 14, 2004: A story is published on WVGhosts.com by a man named Ed Rollins. While visiting an abandoned munitions plant along a creek bank near Bethel Church Road, he saw a huge animal that walked on all fours break the tree line. It was covered in dirty, brownish-yellow, matted fur, had a long pointed head like a dog's but

with small goatlike horns, and had small front paws. The creature drank from the creek then reentered the woods.
Source: *WVGhosts.com*, 2004

Wisconsin
Late 1980s: Ross Tamms and his girlfriend go for an afternoon drive and witness a huge animal kneeling and holding a small dead dog in the yard of a farmhouse near Holy Hill, in the Hubertus area. The huge thing had thick reddish-brown fur, broad shoulders, a short, almost nonexistent neck, and a black face similar to a great ape's. When the animal's scent reached the car it was so strong that the two became nauseated.
Source: *Monsters of Wisconsin*, 2011.

1996: "RAS" watches two six- to seven-foot-tall, bipedal, furry creatures with slanted eyes leave a cemetery and cross Scenic Road very quickly in the Hubertus area of Washington County.
Source: *Strange Wisconsin*, 2004.

Autumn, 2003: Jason Miller sees a strange goatlike humanoid creature in the woods around South Mill Road, also known as Goatman's Road, in Kewaskum. It had the head and arms of a human, a long gray beard, and two goatlike legs. He said the creature was muttering obscenities and had a powerful, nauseating odor.
Source: Author's files.

November, 2004: Rick Selcherk sees a strange animal cross the road in front of him on Highway 60 between Slinger and Mayfield.
Source: *Strange Wisconsin*, 2004.

June, 2006: Three West Bend boys see a large, tailless, doglike creature with glowing red eyes while playing in a wooded area never Silver

Creek. The animal was crouched over a partially eaten small mammal. The height of the animal was estimated to be greater than six feet and four inches.
Source: Author's files.

November 6, 2006: While collecting roadkill for Washington County on Highway 167 near Holy Hill Basilica, Steven Krueger sees a six- or seven-foot-tall creature in his rearview mirror reaching for a dead deer that he'd just placed into the back of the truck.
Source: *Strange Wisconsin*, 2004.

November 7, 2006: Washington County Bigfoot researcher Mike Lane investigates the Highway 167 sighting and finds large, bipedal, undefined footprints, but they are too shallow to cast or describe. He also finds evidence that something large has been sleeping in a hay pile in a nearby barn.
Source: *Strange Wisconsin*, 2004.

November 12, 2006: Two men were driving north down Shalom Drive just outside of West Bend at approximately eight thirty at night, when a large, muscular, furry quadruped shambled across the road in front of them. It had a huge round head, pointed ears, and no tail, and it was the size of a deer.
Source: *Strange Wisconsin*, 2004.

December 25, 2009. Enormous six-toed footprints measuring fifteen inches long heel to toe are photographed in the front of a home located in the woods near Pike Lake, outside of Hartford. The prints are almost immediately destroyed by a light snowfall.
Source: Author's files.

MEDIA GUIDE

In order to make this book enjoyable for both longtime monster buffs and new enthusiasts alike, I've compiled a list of books, websites, and movies that I believe have merit. The resources included in this guide are not all goat-man specific, but would likely prove interesting to anyone interested in monsters, mythology, or urban legend.

Please note that there are many excellence state- and region-specific books dealing with monsters and Fortean topics specific to your area, but they've been excluded from this guide due to space restrictions.

Books (Nonfiction):
America's Nightmare Monsters by Philip Rife. A collection of the most disturbing and unusual monsters said to roam the United States.
Bigfoot: True-Life Encounters with Legendary Ape-Men by Rupert Matthews. An in-depth history of the American Sasquatch.
Half Human Half Animal by Jamie Hall. This book is a collection of shape-shifter legends and myths worldwide.

Hunting the American Werewolf by Linda S. Godfrey. Linda travels the country in search of modern-day wolf-man sightings.

Lizard Man: The True Story of the Bishopville Monster by Lyle Blackburn. A huge reptilian creature stalks the swamps of South Carolina.

Mirabilis: A Carnival of Cryptozoology and Unnatural History by Dr. Karl Shuker. A collection of strange creatures and puzzling phenomena by one of the world's most respected cryptozoologists.

Mothman Prophecies by John Keel. This Fortean classic chronicles a rash of terrifying flying-humanoid sightings that culminated in the deaths of dozens of people when a bridge collapsed over the Ohio River.

Mysterious America by Loren Coleman. The noted cryptozoologist examines some of the most fascinating monsters to ever be sighted in the United States.

Mythical Creatures Bible by Brenda Rosen. A beautifully illustrated handbook of mythical beings from around the world. It's both a great introduction to mythology as well as great reference guide.

Three Men Seeking Monsters by Nick Redfern. A beer-soaked, punk rock–infused journey through Great Britain's monstrous countryside.

Unexplained!: Strange Sightings, Incredible Occurrences, and Puzzling Physical Phenomena by Jerome Clark. This book is an A-Z guide of infamous Fortean phenomena ranging from monsters to UFOs to strange objects falling from the sky.

Vanishing Hitchhiker: American Urban Legends and Their Meanings by Jan H. Brunvand. This book is a thought-provoking investigation into numerous infamous urban legends.

Books (Fiction)

The Bottoms by Joe R. Lansdale. This book is an enthralling mystery inspired by Goatman legends from around Texas. When a series of mysterious murders occurs near infamous Goatman Bridge, the local children suspect it's the work of the local monster, while others begin to suspect members of the local African-American community.

Websites (Listed Alphabetically):
CultOfWeird. The Cult is a one-stop spot for all things bizarre. Content ranges from strange taxidermy and medical anomalies to cryptozoology and hauntings. www.cultofweird.com

CryptoMundo. Perhaps the most respected crypto blog on the Internet, this website features content by the likes of Loren Coleman, Nick Redfern, and other highly respected cryptozoologists and Fortean writers. www.cryptmundo.com

Snopes. Snopes is the foremost debunker of urban legends in the digital age. Did you get a suspicious-looking e-mail this week claiming your congressman likes to dress like a Care Bear and rob liquor stores? Snopes has probably already gotten to the bottom of things. www.snopes.com

Unexplained-Mysteries. This site is a vast depository of Fortean phenomena. It features articles by some of the best Fortean writers as well as an active family of message forums. www.unexplained-mysteries.com

Documentaries

Legend of Boggy Creek, 1972. This film is a Bigfoot documentary that became a drive-in cult classic in the 1970s. *Boggy* examines evidence of Arkansas's infamous Fouke Monster. The film features reenactments as well as numerous interviews with eyewitnesses.

Southern Fried Bigfoot, 2007. This documentary focuses on many of the more famous Bigfoot-like creatures from the Deep South. Many of cryptozoology's leading experts offer evidence and opinions.

Movies (Fiction)

Deadly Detour: The Goatman Murders, 2012. This is a gory little straight-to-video monster movie about a group of kids who encounter Maryland's Goatman en route to Florida for spring break.

Jimmy Tupper vs. the Goatman of Bowie, 2010. Every great monster should star in at least one mockumentary film. This *Paranormal Activity*–style "found footage" horror film follows the titular character when a prank inadvertently puts him in the sights of Maryland's Goatman.

Legend of the Pope Lick Monster, 1988. This black-and-white independent short film chronicles a group of drunken high school students' ill-advised journey onto the Pope Lick Trestle in search of the Sheepman, aka Goatman.

Comic Books

Goatman is the title of an ongoing series of comic books published by writer and artist Tim Vargulish. The series revolves around the comic's titular character as he travels the world to understand who and what he is, and he ends up battling other cryptids along the way. Issues of the series can be bought by writing to Tim at TVargulish@gmail.com with the title "Goatmail."

X-Files #37, February, 1998. In this issue of the long-canceled but highly entertaining series published by the now defunct Topps Comics, Mulder and Scully investigate a series of strange murders in Bowie, Maryland. Mulder is convinced the Goatman is responsible; Scully—surprisingly enough—is skeptical. Available wherever back issues are sold.

SELECTED BIBLIOGRAPHY

"29 Goats Haul Him on Way to Wisconsin." *Racine Journal-Times,* July 22, 1949.

Baccus, Francis. NewAdvent.org. "St. Paul the Hermit." Accessed on April 11, 2014. http://www.newadvent.org/cathen/11590b.htm.

Black, Edwin. HNN.us. "The Horrifying American Roots of Nazi Eugenics." Accessed on January 3, 2014. http://hnn.us/article/1796.

Boeche, Raymond W. "Bipedal Humanoids in Nebraska: A Chronology of Events." *Journal of the Fortean Research Center volume* 2, no. 1, (April, 1987): 4–6.

"Bond Not Yet Fixed for Alleged Slayer of Brother-In-Law." *Denton Record-Chronicle,* October 16, 1917.

Bryant, Judy. "Trestle of Death: Film Depicting Legend Stirs Fear of Life Imitating Art." *The Courier-Journal,* December 30, 1988.

Chandler, Kurt. "Where the Wild Things Are." *Milwaukee Magazine* 36 (2011): 70–76.

Chattin, John. "Film Brings Deadly Legend Alive." *College Heights Herald,* March 28, 1989.

Clarke, Sallie Ann. *The Lake Worth Monster of Greer Island, Fort Worth, Texas.* Fort Worth, TX: self-published, 1969.

Coleman, Loren. *Mysterious America.* Boston, MA: Faber & Faber, 1983.

Couch, J. Nathan. CultOfWeird.com. "Pope Lick Monster." Accessed July 31, 2013.

Couch, J. Nathan. *Washington County Paranormal: A Wisconsin Legend Trip.* West Bend, WI: self-published, 2012.

Crombie, Robert Ogilvie. *The Gentleman and the Faun.* Scotland, UK: Findhorn Press, 2009.

Dager, Wendy. "Over Decades, Ongoing Tales of the Billiwhack Monster of Santa Paula Cast Long Shadows of Doubt." *Ventura County Star,* October 31, 2008.

Daly, Sean. "The Legend of Goatman: P.G. County's Ax-Wielding, Dog-Beheading and Much Loved Urban Legend Makes a 90's Comeback." *The Washington City Paper,* September 18, 1998.

Daniels, Les. *Marvel: Five Fabulous Decades of the World's Greatest Comics.* New York, NY: Harry N. Abrams, 1991.

Gerhard, Ken; and Redfern; Nick. *Monsters of Texas.* North Devon: CFZ Press, 2010.

Geringer, Joseph. CrimeLibrary.com. "The Phantom Killer: Texarkana Moonlight Murders." Accessed on February 9, 2014. http://www.crimelibrary.com/serial_killers/unsolved/texarkana/index_1.html.

"Gets Five-Year Suspended Sentence on Murder Charge." *Galveston Daily News,* April 7, 1919.

Glaze, Michelle P. DentonHistory.net. "The Quakertown Story." Accessed on June 18, 2013. http://dentonhistory.net/page32/Quaker.html.

"Goat Caravan Ordered Off Road." *La Crosse Tribune,* September 9, 1949.

"Goat Drawn Wagon On Way to Florida." *Waukesha Daily Freeman,* February 18, 1950.

Godfrey, Linda S. BeastOfBrayRoad.com. "Sightings Log." Accessed January 2, 2014. http://www.beastofbrayroad.com/sightingslog.html.

Godfrey, Linda S. *Hunting the American Werewolf.* Madison, WI: Trail Book, 2006.

Godfrey, Linda S. *Monsters of Wisconsin.* Mechanicsburg, PA: Stackpole Books, 2011.

Godfrey, Linda S. *Strange Wisconsin: More Badger State Weirdness.* Madison, WI: Trail Book, 2007.

Griesbach, Gay. "Creature's Identity Questioned." *Hartford Times Press,* November 23, 2006.

Griesbach, Gay. "Goatman Goes Environmentalist." *West Bend Daily News,* November 11, 2013.

Gumm, Kayla, and Rayeske, Jenny. Wisconsinosity.com. "Goatman & Hogsback: Where the Real Action Is." Accessed June 27, 2012. http://www.wisconsinosity.com/articles/weird_wi_archived/weirdstories/goatman.htm.

Hall, Mark A. "Satyrs and Centaurs." *Wonders volume 10,* no. 3 (September, 2006) 83-85.

Harris, David Robert. ShawneeGoatIsReal.Blogspot.com. Accessed on July 6, 2012. http://www.shawneegoatisreal.blogspot.com.

Herodotus. *The Histories.* Translated by George Rawlinson. New York, NY: Alfred A. Knopf, 1997.

Hill, Bob. TheParkLands.org. "The Pope Lick Monster." Accessed January 6, 2014. http://www.theparklands.org/Blog/15/THE-POPE-LICK-MONSTER.

Holland, Jeffery S. *Weird Kentucky.* New York, NY: Sterling Publishing Co., Inc., 2008.

Huber, Margaret W. EncyclopediaVirginia.org. "Religion in Early Virginia Indian Society." Accessed on January 2, 2014. http://encyclopediavirginia.org/Religion_in_Early_Virginia_Indian_Society.

Indiana State University Archives. "Arches." Indiana Folklore Collection. http://visions.indstate.edu:8888/cdm/search/collection/folklore/searchterm/arches/order/nosort.

Jackson, Tamilia E. HauntedAmericaTours.com. "The Haunted Troll Bridge of Marshall, Texas!" Accessed on June 18, 2013.

Jenkins, Joseph. FatherJoe.wordpress.com. "The Goatman of Prince George's County." Accessed on December 3, 2013. http://fatherjoe.wordpress.com/stories/the-goatman-of-prince-georges-county/.

Jennings, Damien. HauntedAmericaTours.com. "The Real Goatman and His Kin." Accessed on June 18, 2013.

Jernagan, Jared. "Brazil Teen Dies in Fall from Madison Township Bridge." *Greencastle Banner-Graphic*, June 4, 2012.

Jones, Jim W. "Ghosts Seen on Greer Island." *Fort Worth Star-Telegraph*, July 14, 1969.

Kennedy, Bud. "1969 Lake Worth Monster, Was the "Goat-Man" Hulk or Hoax?." Fort Worth Star-Telegraph, June 8, 2006.

Lake, Matt. *Weird Maryland*. New York, NY: Sterling Publishing Co., Inc., 2006.

"La Porte People Prepare Funeral for Slain Baby." *Galveston Daily News*, April 25, 1950.

Marrs, Jim. "Fishy Man-Goat Terrifies Couples Parked at Lake Worth." *Fort Worth Star-Telegram*, July 10, 1969.

Marrs, Jim. "Police, Residents Observe but Can't Identify 'Monster.'" *Fort Worth Star-Telegram*, July 11, 1969.

Mayor, Adrienne. *The First Fossil Hunters: Paleontology in Greek and Roman Times*. Princeton, NJ: Princeton University Press, 2000.

Mayrick, Thomas. "The Caribees of the Honduras," *The Month 2*, no. 13 (July to December, 1870) 97–103.

McCoy, Kurt. *White Things: West Virginia's Weird White Monsters*. Morgantown, WV: Ogua Books, 2008.

Mela, Pomponius. *Description of the World*. Translated by Frank E. Romer. Ann Arbor, MI: University of Michigan Press, 1998.

Middleton, Megan. "Old Alton Bridge Retains Magnetic Appeal." *Denton Record-Chronicle*, June 10, 2003.

Moran, Rick. "The Old Alton Bridge." *Fate Magazine* 692 (2007) 38–48.

Nichols, Andrew. *Ctesias: On India*. New York, NY: Bloomsbury Academic, 2011.

Noe, Allen V. "And Still the Reports Roll In," *Pursuit* 7, no. 1, (January, 1974): 16–19.

Opsasnick, Mark. *The Maryland Bigfoot Digest*. Xlibris, 2004.

Opsasnick, Mark. *The Real Story Behind the Exorcist: A Study of the Haunted Boy and Other True-Life Horror Legends from Around the Nation's Capital*. Xlibris, 2007.

Patton, Darryl. *America's Goat Man (Mr. Ches McCartney)*. Gadsden, AL: Little River Press, 2003.

PhantomsAndMonsters.com. "The Maryland Goatman Legend." Accessed on January 2, 2014. http://www.phantomsandmonsters.com/2012_08_05_archive.html.

Plutarch. *Lives of Illustrious Men*. Translated by A. H. Clough. Boston, MA: Little, Brown, and Company, 1930.

"Prince Aggie, $110,000 Bull of Billiwhack Stock Farm is Dead; Famous Son Sought by Farm." *Oxnard Daily Courier*, June 15, 1926.

Redfern, Nick. Mania.com. "Coming of the Goatman." Accessed on June 6, 2012. http://www.mania.com/coming-goatman_article_112524.html.

Rush, Steve. "The Monster at Pope Lick." *The New Voice*, October 31, 1990.

Sanderson, Ivan T. *Abominable Snowmen: Legend Come to Life*. Kempton, IL: Adventures Unlimited Press, 2006.

Shuker, Dr. Karl P. N. *Unexplained*. North Dighton, MA: JG Press, Inc., 1996.

Silverstein, Amy. "Ohio River Is the Most Polluted River in the United States." *Global Post*, April 5, 2012.

"Stolen Towel Clew: Murder of Baby Investigated Here." *Galveston Daily News*, April 22, 1950.

Styn, Rebecca. ErieReader.com. "Eerie Erie." Accessed on July 23, 2013. http://www.eriereader.com/article/eerie-erie-.

Suttner, John. "Hundreds, Holding Noses, See Traveling Goat-Man." *Waukesha Daily Freeman*, August 29, 1949.

Swope, Robin. Examiner.com. "The Legend of the Sheepman of Waterford, Pennsylvania." Accessed on July 23, 2013. http://www.examiner.com/article/the-legend-of-the-sheepman-of-waterford-pennsylvania.

TheShadowLands.net. "Haunted Places in Wisconsin." Accessed on January 2, 2014. http://www.theshadowlands.net/places/wisconsin.htm.

Treat, Wesley,; Shade, Heather; and Riggs, Rob. *Weird Texas*. New York, NY: Sterling Publishing Co., Inc., 2005.

Triem, Judith P., and Stone, Mitch. SCVHistory.com. "Rancho Camulos. National Register of Historic Places Nomination." Accessed on January 3, 2014. http://www.scvhistory.com/scvhistory/camulos-nrhp3.htm.

Trimborn, Harry. "There's a Beast at Billiwhack—but Only the Kids Can See Him." *Los Angeles Times*, November 4, 1964.

Tweedale, Violet. *Ghosts I Have Seen and Other Psychic Experiences*. New York, NY: Frederick A. Stokes Company, 1919.

United States Department of Agricultures. "USDA History Exhibit." Accessed January 2, 2014. http://www.ars.usda.gov/Aboutus/docs.htm?docid=8821.

Van Buren, Abigail. "Dear Abby." *Brownsville Herald*, November 8, 1960.

Vaughn, Chris "Mystery Still Engulfs Lake Worth Monster." *NBC-5 Dallas-Fort Worth*, August 8, 2009.

Vergano, Dan. "Mythical Satyr May Be Preserved in Salt." *USA Today*, July 23, 2007.

ABOUT THE AUTHOR

J. Nathan Couch grew up in the foothills of Northeast Georgia's Appalachian Mountains. Given the area's rich tradition of ghost stories and folklore, it's no wonder he developed a passion for the bizarre and the unexplained.

Nathan is currently a resident of West Bend, Wisconsin. His first book, *Washington County Paranormal: A Wisconsin Legend Trip*, was published in 2012, and his fictional short story, *Anna*, appeared in the 2013 WWA Press anthology *A Wisconsin Harvest, Volume II*.

When he isn't writing about ghosts and monsters, he's usually talking about them with Mike Hoke on *The Strange Side with Mike and Nate*, a weekly Internet radio show that airs live each week on ZTalkRadio.com.

Photo by Charlie Hintz of Mental Shed Studios.

ORDERING AND CONTACT INFORMATION

Goatman: Flesh or Folklore? and *Washington County Paranormal* are both available through all major book retailers both nationally and internationally. If you don't have access to mainstream book distribution channels and would like to stock either title in your business or library, please contact the author at JNathanCouch.com for additional information.